C-2675   CAREER EXAMINATION SERIES

This is your
PASSBOOK for...

Community Service Worker

Test Preparation Study Guide
Questions & Answers

NATIONAL LEARNING CORPORATION®

COPYRIGHT NOTICE

This book is SOLELY intended for, is sold ONLY to, and its use is RESTRICTED to individual, bona fide applicants or candidates who qualify by virtue of having seriously filed applications for appropriate license, certificate, professional and/or promotional advancement, higher school matriculation, scholarship, or other legitimate requirements of education and/or governmental authorities.

This book is NOT intended for use, class instruction, tutoring, training, duplication, copying, reprinting, excerption, or adaptation, etc., by:

1) Other publishers
2) Proprietors and/or Instructors of "Coaching" and/or Preparatory Courses
3) Personnel and/or Training Divisions of commercial, industrial, and governmental organizations
4) Schools, colleges, or universities and/or their departments and staffs, including teachers and other personnel
5) Testing Agencies or Bureaus
6) Study groups which seek by the purchase of a single volume to copy and/or duplicate and/or adapt this material for use by the group as a whole without having purchased individual volumes for each of the members of the group
7) Et al.

Such persons would be in violation of appropriate Federal and State statutes.

PROVISION OF LICENSING AGREEMENTS – Recognized educational, commercial, industrial, and governmental institutions and organizations, and others legitimately engaged in educational pursuits, including training, testing, and measurement activities, may address request for a licensing agreement to the copyright owners, who will determine whether, and under what conditions, including fees and charges, the materials in this book may be used them. In other words, a licensing facility exists for the legitimate use of the material in this book on other than an individual basis. However, it is asseverated and affirmed here that the material in this book CANNOT be used without the receipt of the express permission of such a licensing agreement from the Publishers. Inquiries re licensing should be addressed to the company, attention rights and permissions department.

All rights reserved, including the right of reproduction in whole or in part, in any form or by any means, electronic or mechanical, including photocopying, recording, or by any information storage and retrieval system, without permission in writing from the Publisher.

Copyright © 2024 by
National Learning Corporation

212 Michael Drive, Syosset, NY 11791
(516) 921-8888 • www.passbooks.com
E-mail: info@passbooks.com

PUBLISHED IN THE UNITED STATES OF AMERICA

PASSBOOK® SERIES

THE *PASSBOOK® SERIES* has been created to prepare applicants and candidates for the ultimate academic battlefield – the examination room.

At some time in our lives, each and every one of us may be required to take an examination – for validation, matriculation, admission, qualification, registration, certification, or licensure.

Based on the assumption that every applicant or candidate has met the basic formal educational standards, has taken the required number of courses, and read the necessary texts, the *PASSBOOK® SERIES* furnishes the one special preparation which may assure passing with confidence, instead of failing with insecurity. Examination questions – together with answers – are furnished as the basic vehicle for study so that the mysteries of the examination and its compounding difficulties may be eliminated or diminished by a sure method.

This book is meant to help you pass your examination provided that you qualify and are serious in your objective.

The entire field is reviewed through the huge store of content information which is succinctly presented through a provocative and challenging approach – the question-and-answer method.

A climate of success is established by furnishing the correct answers at the end of each test.

You soon learn to recognize types of questions, forms of questions, and patterns of questioning. You may even begin to anticipate expected outcomes.

You perceive that many questions are repeated or adapted so that you can gain acute insights, which may enable you to score many sure points.

You learn how to confront new questions, or types of questions, and to attack them confidently and work out the correct answers.

You note objectives and emphases, and recognize pitfalls and dangers, so that you may make positive educational adjustments.

Moreover, you are kept fully informed in relation to new concepts, methods, practices, and directions in the field.

You discover that you are actually taking the examination all the time: you are preparing for the examination by "taking" an examination, not by reading extraneous and/or supererogatory textbooks.

In short, this PASSBOOK®, used directedly, should be an important factor in helping you to pass your test.

COMMUNITY SERVICE WORKER

DUTIES:
Performs non-professional duties to assist professional social and community workers in the implementation and delivery of agency programs and services. Provides information concerning services offered by public or private agencies. Assists applicants in filling out forms and explains procedures to be followed. Makes routine field visits to gather documentation and obtain information concerning an applicant's eligibility for agency services. Assists in evaluating day care and foster care homes by performing collateral visits to schools and other agencies. Provides transportation for clients in conjunction with the delivery of agency services. Performs related work as required.

EXAMPLES OF WORK: (illustrative only)
- Provides information to individuals or groups concerning services offered by public and private agencies; Assists clients in completing necessary forms, obtaining eligibility information, proof of births, deaths, and marriages;
- Acts as interpreter, if bilingual, to help clients and workers facilitate the intake process;
- May make home visits to follow up on broken appointments or gather routine information;
- Assists clients in areas of housing, employment, school attendance, recreation, money management, day care, transportation, and escort;
- Assists in communication between agency, client, and the community by clarifying agency programs to individuals and conveying community cultural patterns and attitudes to agency professional staff;
- Assists individuals in recognizing conditions contributing to social problems and in making efforts toward correcting these conditions.

SCOPE OF THE EXAMINATION:
The multiple-choice test will cover knowledge, skills and/or abilities in such areas as:
1. **Applying information** - These questions test for the ability to apply simple information. You will be given a Resource Directory that describes community agencies, their purposes and the type of client each serves. Questions describe clients with a variety of problems and situations. You must determine the appropriate referral for clients based on the services which each agency provides.
2. **Educating and interacting with the public** - These questions test for knowledge of techniques used to interact effectively with individual citizens and/or community groups, to educate or inform them about topics of concern, to publicize or clarify agency programs or policies, to negotiate conflicts or resolve complaints, and to represent one's agency or program in a manner in keeping with good public relations practices. Questions may also cover interacting with others in cooperative efforts of public outreach or service.
3. **Interviewing** - These questions test for knowledge of the principles and practices employed in obtaining information from individuals through structured conversations. These questions require you to apply the principles, practices, and techniques of effective interviewing to hypothetical interviewing situations. Included are questions that present a problem arising from an interviewing situation, and you must choose the most appropriate course of action to take.
4. **Working with people in human services situations** - These questions test for knowledge of general techniques used to deal with common client behaviors such as fear, hostility, shyness, resistance, defensiveness, withdrawal, anxiety and confusion.

HOW TO TAKE A TEST

I. YOU MUST PASS AN EXAMINATION

A. WHAT EVERY CANDIDATE SHOULD KNOW

Examination applicants often ask us for help in preparing for the written test. What can I study in advance? What kinds of questions will be asked? How will the test be given? How will the papers be graded?

As an applicant for a civil service examination, you may be wondering about some of these things. Our purpose here is to suggest effective methods of advance study and to describe civil service examinations.

Your chances for success on this examination can be increased if you know how to prepare. Those "pre-examination jitters" can be reduced if you know what to expect. You can even experience an adventure in good citizenship if you know why civil service exams are given.

B. WHY ARE CIVIL SERVICE EXAMINATIONS GIVEN?

Civil service examinations are important to you in two ways. As a citizen, you want public jobs filled by employees who know how to do their work. As a job seeker, you want a fair chance to compete for that job on an equal footing with other candidates. The best-known means of accomplishing this two-fold goal is the competitive examination.

Exams are widely publicized throughout the nation. They may be administered for jobs in federal, state, city, municipal, town or village governments or agencies.

Any citizen may apply, with some limitations, such as the age or residence of applicants. Your experience and education may be reviewed to see whether you meet the requirements for the particular examination. When these requirements exist, they are reasonable and applied consistently to all applicants. Thus, a competitive examination may cause you some uneasiness now, but it is your privilege and safeguard.

C. HOW ARE CIVIL SERVICE EXAMS DEVELOPED?

Examinations are carefully written by trained technicians who are specialists in the field known as "psychological measurement," in consultation with recognized authorities in the field of work that the test will cover. These experts recommend the subject matter areas or skills to be tested; only those knowledges or skills important to your success on the job are included. The most reliable books and source materials available are used as references. Together, the experts and technicians judge the difficulty level of the questions.

Test technicians know how to phrase questions so that the problem is clearly stated. Their ethics do not permit "trick" or "catch" questions. Questions may have been tried out on sample groups, or subjected to statistical analysis, to determine their usefulness.

Written tests are often used in combination with performance tests, ratings of training and experience, and oral interviews. All of these measures combine to form the best-known means of finding the right person for the right job.

II. HOW TO PASS THE WRITTEN TEST

A. NATURE OF THE EXAMINATION

To prepare intelligently for civil service examinations, you should know how they differ from school examinations you have taken. In school you were assigned certain definite pages to read or subjects to cover. The examination questions were quite detailed and usually emphasized memory. Civil service exams, on the other hand, try to discover your present ability to perform the duties of a position, plus your potentiality to learn these duties. In other words, a civil service exam attempts to predict how successful you will be. Questions cover such a broad area that they cannot be as minute and detailed as school exam questions.

In the public service similar kinds of work, or positions, are grouped together in one "class." This process is known as *position-classification*. All the positions in a class are paid according to the salary range for that class. One class title covers all of these positions, and they are all tested by the same examination.

B. FOUR BASIC STEPS

1) Study the announcement

How, then, can you know what subjects to study? Our best answer is: "Learn as much as possible about the class of positions for which you've applied." The exam will test the knowledge, skills and abilities needed to do the work.

Your most valuable source of information about the position you want is the official exam announcement. This announcement lists the training and experience qualifications. Check these standards and apply only if you come reasonably close to meeting them.

The brief description of the position in the examination announcement offers some clues to the subjects which will be tested. Think about the job itself. Review the duties in your mind. Can you perform them, or are there some in which you are rusty? Fill in the blank spots in your preparation.

Many jurisdictions preview the written test in the exam announcement by including a section called "Knowledge and Abilities Required," "Scope of the Examination," or some similar heading. Here you will find out specifically what fields will be tested.

2) Review your own background

Once you learn in general what the position is all about, and what you need to know to do the work, ask yourself which subjects you already know fairly well and which need improvement. You may wonder whether to concentrate on improving your strong areas or on building some background in your fields of weakness. When the announcement has specified "some knowledge" or "considerable knowledge," or has used adjectives like "beginning principles of…" or "advanced … methods," you can get a clue as to the number and difficulty of questions to be asked in any given field. More questions, and hence broader coverage, would be included for those subjects which are more important in the work. Now weigh your strengths and weaknesses against the job requirements and prepare accordingly.

3) Determine the level of the position

Another way to tell how intensively you should prepare is to understand the level of the job for which you are applying. Is it the entering level? In other words, is this the position in which beginners in a field of work are hired? Or is it an intermediate or advanced level? Sometimes this is indicated by such words as "Junior" or "Senior" in the class title. Other jurisdictions use Roman numerals to designate the level – Clerk I, Clerk II, for example. The word "Supervisor" sometimes appears in the title. If the level is not indicated by the title, check the description of duties. Will you be working under very close supervision, or will you have responsibility for independent decisions in this work?

4) Choose appropriate study materials

Now that you know the subjects to be examined and the relative amount of each subject to be covered, you can choose suitable study materials. For beginning level jobs, or even advanced ones, if you have a pronounced weakness in some aspect of your training, read a modern, standard textbook in that field. Be sure it is up to date and has general coverage. Such books are normally available at your library, and the librarian will be glad to help you locate one. For entry-level positions, questions of appropriate difficulty are chosen – neither highly advanced questions, nor those too simple. Such questions require careful thought but not advanced training.

If the position for which you are applying is technical or advanced, you will read more advanced, specialized material. If you are already familiar with the basic principles of your field, elementary textbooks would waste your time. Concentrate on advanced textbooks and technical periodicals. Think through the concepts and review difficult problems in your field.

These are all general sources. You can get more ideas on your own initiative, following these leads. For example, training manuals and publications of the government agency which employs workers in your field can be useful, particularly for technical and professional positions. A letter or visit to the government department involved may result in more specific study suggestions, and certainly will provide you with a more definite idea of the exact nature of the position you are seeking.

III. KINDS OF TESTS

Tests are used for purposes other than measuring knowledge and ability to perform specified duties. For some positions, it is equally important to test ability to make adjustments to new situations or to profit from training. In others, basic mental abilities not dependent on information are essential. Questions which test these things may not appear as pertinent to the duties of the position as those which test for knowledge and information. Yet they are often highly important parts of a fair examination. For very general questions, it is almost impossible to help you direct your study efforts. What we can do is to point out some of the more common of these general abilities needed in public service positions and describe some typical questions.

1) General information

Broad, general information has been found useful for predicting job success in some kinds of work. This is tested in a variety of ways, from vocabulary lists to questions about current events. Basic background in some field of work, such as sociology or economics, may be sampled in a group of questions. Often these are principles which have become familiar to most persons through exposure rather than through formal training. It is difficult to advise you how to study for these questions; being alert to the world around you is our best suggestion.

2) Verbal ability

An example of an ability needed in many positions is verbal or language ability. Verbal ability is, in brief, the ability to use and understand words. Vocabulary and grammar tests are typical measures of this ability. Reading comprehension or paragraph interpretation questions are common in many kinds of civil service tests. You are given a paragraph of written material and asked to find its central meaning.

3) Numerical ability

Number skills can be tested by the familiar arithmetic problem, by checking paired lists of numbers to see which are alike and which are different, or by interpreting charts and graphs. In the latter test, a graph may be printed in the test booklet which you are asked to use as the basis for answering questions.

4) Observation

A popular test for law-enforcement positions is the observation test. A picture is shown to you for several minutes, then taken away. Questions about the picture test your ability to observe both details and larger elements.

5) Following directions

In many positions in the public service, the employee must be able to carry out written instructions dependably and accurately. You may be given a chart with several columns, each column listing a variety of information. The questions require you to carry out directions involving the information given in the chart.

6) Skills and aptitudes

Performance tests effectively measure some manual skills and aptitudes. When the skill is one in which you are trained, such as typing or shorthand, you can practice. These tests are often very much like those given in business school or high school courses. For many of the other skills and aptitudes, however, no short-time preparation can be made. Skills and abilities natural to you or that you have developed throughout your lifetime are being tested.

Many of the general questions just described provide all the data needed to answer the questions and ask you to use your reasoning ability to find the answers. Your best preparation for these tests, as well as for tests of facts and ideas, is to be at your physical and mental best. You, no doubt, have your own methods of getting into an exam-taking mood and keeping "in shape." The next section lists some ideas on this subject.

IV. KINDS OF QUESTIONS

Only rarely is the "essay" question, which you answer in narrative form, used in civil service tests. Civil service tests are usually of the short-answer type. Full instructions for answering these questions will be given to you at the examination. But in case this is your first experience with short-answer questions and separate answer sheets, here is what you need to know:

1) **Multiple-choice Questions**

Most popular of the short-answer questions is the "multiple choice" or "best answer" question. It can be used, for example, to test for factual knowledge, ability to solve problems or judgment in meeting situations found at work.

A multiple-choice question is normally one of three types—
- It can begin with an incomplete statement followed by several possible endings. You are to find the one ending which *best* completes the statement, although some of the others may not be entirely wrong.
- It can also be a complete statement in the form of a question which is answered by choosing one of the statements listed.

- It can be in the form of a problem – again you select the best answer.

Here is an example of a multiple-choice question with a discussion which should give you some clues as to the method for choosing the right answer:

When an employee has a complaint about his assignment, the action which will *best* help him overcome his difficulty is to
  A. discuss his difficulty with his coworkers
  B. take the problem to the head of the organization
  C. take the problem to the person who gave him the assignment
  D. say nothing to anyone about his complaint

In answering this question, you should study each of the choices to find which is best. Consider choice "A" – Certainly an employee may discuss his complaint with fellow employees, but no change or improvement can result, and the complaint remains unresolved. Choice "B" is a poor choice since the head of the organization probably does not know what assignment you have been given, and taking your problem to him is known as "going over the head" of the supervisor. The supervisor, or person who made the assignment, is the person who can clarify it or correct any injustice. Choice "C" is, therefore, correct. To say nothing, as in choice "D," is unwise. Supervisors have and interest in knowing the problems employees are facing, and the employee is seeking a solution to his problem.

2) True/False Questions

The "true/false" or "right/wrong" form of question is sometimes used. Here a complete statement is given. Your job is to decide whether the statement is right or wrong.

SAMPLE: A roaming cell-phone call to a nearby city costs less than a non-roaming call to a distant city.

This statement is wrong, or false, since roaming calls are more expensive.
This is not a complete list of all possible question forms, although most of the others are variations of these common types. You will always get complete directions for answering questions. Be sure you understand *how* to mark your answers – ask questions until you do.

V. RECORDING YOUR ANSWERS

Computer terminals are used more and more today for many different kinds of exams.
For an examination with very few applicants, you may be told to record your answers in the test booklet itself. Separate answer sheets are much more common. If this separate answer sheet is to be scored by machine – and this is often the case – it is highly important that you mark your answers correctly in order to get credit.
An electronic scoring machine is often used in civil service offices because of the speed with which papers can be scored. Machine-scored answer sheets must be marked with a pencil, which will be given to you. This pencil has a high graphite content which responds to the electronic scoring machine. As a matter of fact, stray dots may register as answers, so do not let your pencil rest on the answer sheet while you are pondering the correct answer. Also, if your pencil lead breaks or is otherwise defective, ask for another.

Since the answer sheet will be dropped in a slot in the scoring machine, be careful not to bend the corners or get the paper crumpled.

The answer sheet normally has five vertical columns of numbers, with 30 numbers to a column. These numbers correspond to the question numbers in your test booklet. After each number, going across the page are four or five pairs of dotted lines. These short dotted lines have small letters or numbers above them. The first two pairs may also have a "T" or "F" above the letters. This indicates that the first two pairs only are to be used if the questions are of the true-false type. If the questions are multiple choice, disregard the "T" and "F" and pay attention only to the small letters or numbers.

Answer your questions in the manner of the sample that follows:

32. The largest city in the United States is
    A. Washington, D.C.
    B. New York City
    C. Chicago
    D. Detroit
    E. San Francisco

1) Choose the answer you think is best. (New York City is the largest, so "B" is correct.)
2) Find the row of dotted lines numbered the same as the question you are answering. (Find row number 32)
3) Find the pair of dotted lines corresponding to the answer. (Find the pair of lines under the mark "B.")
4) Make a solid black mark between the dotted lines.

VI. BEFORE THE TEST

Common sense will help you find procedures to follow to get ready for an examination. Too many of us, however, overlook these sensible measures. Indeed, nervousness and fatigue have been found to be the most serious reasons why applicants fail to do their best on civil service tests. Here is a list of reminders:

- Begin your preparation early – Don't wait until the last minute to go scurrying around for books and materials or to find out what the position is all about.
- Prepare continuously – An hour a night for a week is better than an all-night cram session. This has been definitely established. What is more, a night a week for a month will return better dividends than crowding your study into a shorter period of time.
- Locate the place of the exam – You have been sent a notice telling you when and where to report for the examination. If the location is in a different town or otherwise unfamiliar to you, it would be well to inquire the best route and learn something about the building.
- Relax the night before the test – Allow your mind to rest. Do not study at all that night. Plan some mild recreation or diversion; then go to bed early and get a good night's sleep.
- Get up early enough to make a leisurely trip to the place for the test – This way unforeseen events, traffic snarls, unfamiliar buildings, etc. will not upset you.
- Dress comfortably – A written test is not a fashion show. You will be known by number and not by name, so wear something comfortable.

- Leave excess paraphernalia at home – Shopping bags and odd bundles will get in your way. You need bring only the items mentioned in the official notice you received; usually everything you need is provided. Do not bring reference books to the exam. They will only confuse those last minutes and be taken away from you when in the test room.
- Arrive somewhat ahead of time – If because of transportation schedules you must get there very early, bring a newspaper or magazine to take your mind off yourself while waiting.
- Locate the examination room – When you have found the proper room, you will be directed to the seat or part of the room where you will sit. Sometimes you are given a sheet of instructions to read while you are waiting. Do not fill out any forms until you are told to do so; just read them and be prepared.
- Relax and prepare to listen to the instructions
- If you have any physical problem that may keep you from doing your best, be sure to tell the test administrator. If you are sick or in poor health, you really cannot do your best on the exam. You can come back and take the test some other time.

VII. AT THE TEST

The day of the test is here and you have the test booklet in your hand. The temptation to get going is very strong. Caution! There is more to success than knowing the right answers. You must know how to identify your papers and understand variations in the type of short-answer question used in this particular examination. Follow these suggestions for maximum results from your efforts:

1) Cooperate with the monitor

The test administrator has a duty to create a situation in which you can be as much at ease as possible. He will give instructions, tell you when to begin, check to see that you are marking your answer sheet correctly, and so on. He is not there to guard you, although he will see that your competitors do not take unfair advantage. He wants to help you do your best.

2) Listen to all instructions

Don't jump the gun! Wait until you understand all directions. In most civil service tests you get more time than you need to answer the questions. So don't be in a hurry. Read each word of instructions until you clearly understand the meaning. Study the examples, listen to all announcements and follow directions. Ask questions if you do not understand what to do.

3) Identify your papers

Civil service exams are usually identified by number only. You will be assigned a number; you must not put your name on your test papers. Be sure to copy your number correctly. Since more than one exam may be given, copy your exact examination title.

4) Plan your time

Unless you are told that a test is a "speed" or "rate of work" test, speed itself is usually not important. Time enough to answer all the questions will be provided, but this does not mean that you have all day. An overall time limit has been set. Divide the total time (in minutes) by the number of questions to determine the approximate time you have for each question.

5) Do not linger over difficult questions

If you come across a difficult question, mark it with a paper clip (useful to have along) and come back to it when you have been through the booklet. One caution if you do this – be sure to skip a number on your answer sheet as well. Check often to be sure that you have not lost your place and that you are marking in the row numbered the same as the question you are answering.

6) Read the questions

Be sure you know what the question asks! Many capable people are unsuccessful because they failed to *read* the questions correctly.

7) Answer all questions

Unless you have been instructed that a penalty will be deducted for incorrect answers, it is better to guess than to omit a question.

8) Speed tests

It is often better NOT to guess on speed tests. It has been found that on timed tests people are tempted to spend the last few seconds before time is called in marking answers at random – without even reading them – in the hope of picking up a few extra points. To discourage this practice, the instructions may warn you that your score will be "corrected" for guessing. That is, a penalty will be applied. The incorrect answers will be deducted from the correct ones, or some other penalty formula will be used.

9) Review your answers

If you finish before time is called, go back to the questions you guessed or omitted to give them further thought. Review other answers if you have time.

10) Return your test materials

If you are ready to leave before others have finished or time is called, take ALL your materials to the monitor and leave quietly. Never take any test material with you. The monitor can discover whose papers are not complete, and taking a test booklet may be grounds for disqualification.

VIII. EXAMINATION TECHNIQUES

1) Read the general instructions carefully. These are usually printed on the first page of the exam booklet. As a rule, these instructions refer to the timing of the examination; the fact that you should not start work until the signal and must stop work at a signal, etc. If there are any *special* instructions, such as a choice of questions to be answered, make sure that you note this instruction carefully.

2) When you are ready to start work on the examination, that is as soon as the signal has been given, read the instructions to each question booklet, underline any key words or phrases, such as *least, best, outline, describe* and the like. In this way you will tend to answer as requested rather than discover on reviewing your paper that you *listed without describing*, that you selected the *worst* choice rather than the *best* choice, etc.

3) If the examination is of the objective or multiple-choice type – that is, each question will also give a series of possible answers: A, B, C or D, and you are called upon to select the best answer and write the letter next to that answer on your answer paper – it is advisable to start answering each question in turn. There may be anywhere from 50 to 100 such questions in the three or four hours allotted and you can see how much time would be taken if you read through all the questions before beginning to answer any. Furthermore, if you come across a question or group of questions which you know would be difficult to answer, it would undoubtedly affect your handling of all the other questions.

4) If the examination is of the essay type and contains but a few questions, it is a moot point as to whether you should read all the questions before starting to answer any one. Of course, if you are given a choice – say five out of seven and the like – then it is essential to read all the questions so you can eliminate the two that are most difficult. If, however, you are asked to answer all the questions, there may be danger in trying to answer the easiest one first because you may find that you will spend too much time on it. The best technique is to answer the first question, then proceed to the second, etc.

5) Time your answers. Before the exam begins, write down the time it started, then add the time allowed for the examination and write down the time it must be completed, then divide the time available somewhat as follows:
    - If 3-1/2 hours are allowed, that would be 210 minutes. If you have 80 objective-type questions, that would be an average of 2-1/2 minutes per question. Allow yourself no more than 2 minutes per question, or a total of 160 minutes, which will permit about 50 minutes to review.
    - If for the time allotment of 210 minutes there are 7 essay questions to answer, that would average about 30 minutes a question. Give yourself only 25 minutes per question so that you have about 35 minutes to review.

6) The most important instruction is to *read each question* and make sure you know what is wanted. The second most important instruction is to *time yourself properly* so that you answer every question. The third most important instruction is to *answer every question*. Guess if you have to but include something for each question. Remember that you will receive no credit for a blank and will probably receive some credit if you write something in answer to an essay question. If you guess a letter – say "B" for a multiple-choice question – you may have guessed right. If you leave a blank as an answer to a multiple-choice question, the examiners may respect your feelings but it will not add a point to your score. Some exams may penalize you for wrong answers, so in such cases *only*, you may not want to guess unless you have some basis for your answer.

7) Suggestions
    a. Objective-type questions
        1. Examine the question booklet for proper sequence of pages and questions
        2. Read all instructions carefully
        3. Skip any question which seems too difficult; return to it after all other questions have been answered
        4. Apportion your time properly; do not spend too much time on any single question or group of questions

5. Note and underline key words – *all, most, fewest, least, best, worst, same, opposite*, etc.
6. Pay particular attention to negatives
7. Note unusual option, e.g., unduly long, short, complex, different or similar in content to the body of the question
8. Observe the use of "hedging" words – *probably, may, most likely*, etc.
9. Make sure that your answer is put next to the same number as the question
10. Do not second-guess unless you have good reason to believe the second answer is definitely more correct
11. Cross out original answer if you decide another answer is more accurate; do not erase until you are ready to hand your paper in
12. Answer all questions; guess unless instructed otherwise
13. Leave time for review

b. Essay questions
1. Read each question carefully
2. Determine exactly what is wanted. Underline key words or phrases.
3. Decide on outline or paragraph answer
4. Include many different points and elements unless asked to develop any one or two points or elements
5. Show impartiality by giving pros and cons unless directed to select one side only
6. Make and write down any assumptions you find necessary to answer the questions
7. Watch your English, grammar, punctuation and choice of words
8. Time your answers; don't crowd material

8) Answering the essay question

Most essay questions can be answered by framing the specific response around several key words or ideas. Here are a few such key words or ideas:

M's: manpower, materials, methods, money, management
P's: purpose, program, policy, plan, procedure, practice, problems, pitfalls, personnel, public relations

a. Six basic steps in handling problems:
1. Preliminary plan and background development
2. Collect information, data and facts
3. Analyze and interpret information, data and facts
4. Analyze and develop solutions as well as make recommendations
5. Prepare report and sell recommendations
6. Install recommendations and follow up effectiveness

b. Pitfalls to avoid
1. *Taking things for granted* – A statement of the situation does not necessarily imply that each of the elements is necessarily true; for example, a complaint may be invalid and biased so that all that can be taken for granted is that a complaint has been registered

2. *Considering only one side of a situation* – Wherever possible, indicate several alternatives and then point out the reasons you selected the best one
3. *Failing to indicate follow up* – Whenever your answer indicates action on your part, make certain that you will take proper follow-up action to see how successful your recommendations, procedures or actions turn out to be
4. *Taking too long in answering any single question* – Remember to time your answers properly

IX. AFTER THE TEST

Scoring procedures differ in detail among civil service jurisdictions although the general principles are the same. Whether the papers are hand-scored or graded by machine we have described, they are nearly always graded by number. That is, the person who marks the paper knows only the number – never the name – of the applicant. Not until all the papers have been graded will they be matched with names. If other tests, such as training and experience or oral interview ratings have been given, scores will be combined. Different parts of the examination usually have different weights. For example, the written test might count 60 percent of the final grade, and a rating of training and experience 40 percent. In many jurisdictions, veterans will have a certain number of points added to their grades.

After the final grade has been determined, the names are placed in grade order and an eligible list is established. There are various methods for resolving ties between those who get the same final grade – probably the most common is to place first the name of the person whose application was received first. Job offers are made from the eligible list in the order the names appear on it. You will be notified of your grade and your rank as soon as all these computations have been made. This will be done as rapidly as possible.

People who are found to meet the requirements in the announcement are called "eligibles." Their names are put on a list of eligible candidates. An eligible's chances of getting a job depend on how high he stands on this list and how fast agencies are filling jobs from the list.

When a job is to be filled from a list of eligibles, the agency asks for the names of people on the list of eligibles for that job. When the civil service commission receives this request, it sends to the agency the names of the three people highest on this list. Or, if the job to be filled has specialized requirements, the office sends the agency the names of the top three persons who meet these requirements from the general list.

The appointing officer makes a choice from among the three people whose names were sent to him. If the selected person accepts the appointment, the names of the others are put back on the list to be considered for future openings.

That is the rule in hiring from all kinds of eligible lists, whether they are for typist, carpenter, chemist, or something else. For every vacancy, the appointing officer has his choice of any one of the top three eligibles on the list. This explains why the person whose name is on top of the list sometimes does not get an appointment when some of the persons lower on the list do. If the appointing officer chooses the second or third eligible, the No. 1 eligible does not get a job at once, but stays on the list until he is appointed or the list is terminated.

X. HOW TO PASS THE INTERVIEW TEST

The examination for which you applied requires an oral interview test. You have already taken the written test and you are now being called for the interview test – the final part of the formal examination.

You may think that it is not possible to prepare for an interview test and that there are no procedures to follow during an interview. Our purpose is to point out some things you can do in advance that will help you and some good rules to follow and pitfalls to avoid while you are being interviewed.

What is an interview supposed to test?

The written examination is designed to test the technical knowledge and competence of the candidate; the oral is designed to evaluate intangible qualities, not readily measured otherwise, and to establish a list showing the relative fitness of each candidate – as measured against his competitors – for the position sought. Scoring is not on the basis of "right" and "wrong," but on a sliding scale of values ranging from "not passable" to "outstanding." As a matter of fact, it is possible to achieve a relatively low score without a single "incorrect" answer because of evident weakness in the qualities being measured.

Occasionally, an examination may consist entirely of an oral test – either an individual or a group oral. In such cases, information is sought concerning the technical knowledges and abilities of the candidate, since there has been no written examination for this purpose. More commonly, however, an oral test is used to supplement a written examination.

Who conducts interviews?

The composition of oral boards varies among different jurisdictions. In nearly all, a representative of the personnel department serves as chairman. One of the members of the board may be a representative of the department in which the candidate would work. In some cases, "outside experts" are used, and, frequently, a businessman or some other representative of the general public is asked to serve. Labor and management or other special groups may be represented. The aim is to secure the services of experts in the appropriate field.

However the board is composed, it is a good idea (and not at all improper or unethical) to ascertain in advance of the interview who the members are and what groups they represent. When you are introduced to them, you will have some idea of their backgrounds and interests, and at least you will not stutter and stammer over their names.

What should be done before the interview?

While knowledge about the board members is useful and takes some of the surprise element out of the interview, there is other preparation which is more substantive. It *is* possible to prepare for an oral interview – in several ways:

1) Keep a copy of your application and review it carefully before the interview

This may be the only document before the oral board, and the starting point of the interview. Know what education and experience you have listed there, and the sequence and dates of all of it. Sometimes the board will ask you to review the highlights of your experience for them; you should not have to hem and haw doing it.

2) Study the class specification and the examination announcement

Usually, the oral board has one or both of these to guide them. The qualities, characteristics or knowledges required by the position sought are stated in these documents. They offer valuable clues as to the nature of the oral interview. For example, if the job involves supervisory responsibilities, the announcement will usually indicate that knowledge of modern supervisory methods and the qualifications of the candidate as a supervisor will be tested. If so, you can expect such questions, frequently in the form of a hypothetical situation which you are expected to solve. NEVER go into an oral without knowledge of the duties and responsibilities of the job you seek.

3) Think through each qualification required

Try to visualize the kind of questions you would ask if you were a board member. How well could you answer them? Try especially to appraise your own knowledge and background in each area, *measured against the job sought*, and identify any areas in which you are weak. Be critical and realistic – do not flatter yourself.

4) Do some general reading in areas in which you feel you may be weak

For example, if the job involves supervision and your past experience has NOT, some general reading in supervisory methods and practices, particularly in the field of human relations, might be useful. Do NOT study agency procedures or detailed manuals. The oral board will be testing your understanding and capacity, not your memory.

5) Get a good night's sleep and watch your general health and mental attitude

You will want a clear head at the interview. Take care of a cold or any other minor ailment, and of course, no hangovers.

What should be done on the day of the interview?

Now comes the day of the interview itself. Give yourself plenty of time to get there. Plan to arrive somewhat ahead of the scheduled time, particularly if your appointment is in the fore part of the day. If a previous candidate fails to appear, the board might be ready for you a bit early. By early afternoon an oral board is almost invariably behind schedule if there are many candidates, and you may have to wait. Take along a book or magazine to read, or your application to review, but leave any extraneous material in the waiting room when you go in for your interview. In any event, relax and compose yourself.

The matter of dress is important. The board is forming impressions about you – from your experience, your manners, your attitude, and your appearance. Give your personal appearance careful attention. Dress your best, but not your flashiest. Choose conservative, appropriate clothing, and be sure it is immaculate. This is a business interview, and your appearance should indicate that you regard it as such. Besides, being well groomed and properly dressed will help boost your confidence.

Sooner or later, someone will call your name and escort you into the interview room. *This is it.* From here on you are on your own. It is too late for any more preparation. But remember, you asked for this opportunity to prove your fitness, and you are here because your request was granted.

What happens when you go in?

The usual sequence of events will be as follows: The clerk (who is often the board stenographer) will introduce you to the chairman of the oral board, who will introduce you to the other members of the board. Acknowledge the introductions before you sit down. Do not be surprised if you find a microphone facing you or a stenotypist sitting by. Oral interviews are usually recorded in the event of an appeal or other review.

Usually the chairman of the board will open the interview by reviewing the highlights of your education and work experience from your application – primarily for the benefit of the other members of the board, as well as to get the material into the record. Do not interrupt or comment unless there is an error or significant misinterpretation; if that is the case, do not hesitate. But do not quibble about insignificant matters. Also, he will usually ask you some question about your education, experience or your present job – partly to get you to start talking and to establish the interviewing "rapport." He may start the actual questioning, or turn it over to one of the other members. Frequently, each member undertakes the questioning on a particular area, one in which he is perhaps most competent, so you can expect each member to participate in the examination. Because time is limited, you may also expect some rather abrupt switches in the direction the questioning takes, so do not be upset by it. Normally, a board member will not pursue a single line of questioning unless he discovers a particular strength or weakness.

After each member has participated, the chairman will usually ask whether any member has any further questions, then will ask you if you have anything you wish to add. Unless you are expecting this question, it may floor you. Worse, it may start you off on an extended, extemporaneous speech. The board is not usually seeking more information. The question is principally to offer you a last opportunity to present further qualifications or to indicate that you have nothing to add. So, if you feel that a significant qualification or characteristic has been overlooked, it is proper to point it out in a sentence or so. Do not compliment the board on the thoroughness of their examination – they have been sketchy, and you know it. If you wish, merely say, "No thank you, I have nothing further to add." This is a point where you can "talk yourself out" of a good impression or fail to present an important bit of information. Remember, *you close the interview yourself*.

The chairman will then say, "That is all, Mr. _____, thank you." Do not be startled; the interview is over, and quicker than you think. Thank him, gather your belongings and take your leave. Save your sigh of relief for the other side of the door.

How to put your best foot forward

Throughout this entire process, you may feel that the board individually and collectively is trying to pierce your defenses, seek out your hidden weaknesses and embarrass and confuse you. Actually, this is not true. They are obliged to make an appraisal of your qualifications for the job you are seeking, and they want to see you in your best light. Remember, they must interview all candidates and a non-cooperative candidate may become a failure in spite of their best efforts to bring out his qualifications. Here are 15 suggestions that will help you:

1) Be natural – Keep your attitude confident, not cocky

If you are not confident that you can do the job, do not expect the board to be. Do not apologize for your weaknesses, try to bring out your strong points. The board is interested in a positive, not negative, presentation. Cockiness will antagonize any board member and make him wonder if you are covering up a weakness by a false show of strength.

2) Get comfortable, but don't lounge or sprawl

Sit erectly but not stiffly. A careless posture may lead the board to conclude that you are careless in other things, or at least that you are not impressed by the importance of the occasion. Either conclusion is natural, even if incorrect. Do not fuss with your clothing, a pencil or an ashtray. Your hands may occasionally be useful to emphasize a point; do not let them become a point of distraction.

3) Do not wisecrack or make small talk

This is a serious situation, and your attitude should show that you consider it as such. Further, the time of the board is limited – they do not want to waste it, and neither should you.

4) Do not exaggerate your experience or abilities

In the first place, from information in the application or other interviews and sources, the board may know more about you than you think. Secondly, you probably will not get away with it. An experienced board is rather adept at spotting such a situation, so do not take the chance.

5) If you know a board member, do not make a point of it, yet do not hide it

Certainly you are not fooling him, and probably not the other members of the board. Do not try to take advantage of your acquaintanceship – it will probably do you little good.

6) Do not dominate the interview

Let the board do that. They will give you the clues – do not assume that you have to do all the talking. Realize that the board has a number of questions to ask you, and do not try to take up all the interview time by showing off your extensive knowledge of the answer to the first one.

7) Be attentive

You only have 20 minutes or so, and you should keep your attention at its sharpest throughout. When a member is addressing a problem or question to you, give him your undivided attention. Address your reply principally to him, but do not exclude the other board members.

8) Do not interrupt

A board member may be stating a problem for you to analyze. He will ask you a question when the time comes. Let him state the problem, and wait for the question.

9) Make sure you understand the question

Do not try to answer until you are sure what the question is. If it is not clear, restate it in your own words or ask the board member to clarify it for you. However, do not haggle about minor elements.

10) Reply promptly but not hastily

A common entry on oral board rating sheets is "candidate responded readily," or "candidate hesitated in replies." Respond as promptly and quickly as you can, but do not jump to a hasty, ill-considered answer.

11) Do not be peremptory in your answers

A brief answer is proper – but do not fire your answer back. That is a losing game from your point of view. The board member can probably ask questions much faster than you can answer them.

12) Do not try to create the answer you think the board member wants

He is interested in what kind of mind you have and how it works – not in playing games. Furthermore, he can usually spot this practice and will actually grade you down on it.

13) Do not switch sides in your reply merely to agree with a board member

Frequently, a member will take a contrary position merely to draw you out and to see if you are willing and able to defend your point of view. Do not start a debate, yet do not surrender a good position. If a position is worth taking, it is worth defending.

14) Do not be afraid to admit an error in judgment if you are shown to be wrong

The board knows that you are forced to reply without any opportunity for careful consideration. Your answer may be demonstrably wrong. If so, admit it and get on with the interview.

15) Do not dwell at length on your present job

The opening question may relate to your present assignment. Answer the question but do not go into an extended discussion. You are being examined for a *new* job, not your present one. As a matter of fact, try to phrase ALL your answers in terms of the job for which you are being examined.

Basis of Rating

Probably you will forget most of these "do's" and "don'ts" when you walk into the oral interview room. Even remembering them all will not ensure you a passing grade. Perhaps you did not have the qualifications in the first place. But remembering them will help you to put your best foot forward, without treading on the toes of the board members.

Rumor and popular opinion to the contrary notwithstanding, an oral board wants you to make the best appearance possible. They know you are under pressure – but they also want to see how you respond to it as a guide to what your reaction would be under the pressures of the job you seek. They will be influenced by the degree of poise you display, the personal traits you show and the manner in which you respond.

ABOUT THIS BOOK

This book contains tests divided into Examination Sections. Go through each test, answering every question in the margin. We have also attached a sample answer sheet at the back of the book that can be removed and used. At the end of each test look at the answer key and check your answers. On the ones you got wrong, look at the right answer choice and learn. Do not fill in the answers first. Do not memorize the questions and answers, but understand the answer and principles involved. On your test, the questions will likely be different from the samples. Questions are changed and new ones added. If you understand these past questions you should have success with any changes that arise. Tests may consist of several types of questions. We have additional books on each subject should more study be advisable or necessary for you. Finally, the more you study, the better prepared you will be. This book is intended to be the last thing you study before you walk into the examination room. Prior study of relevant texts is also recommended. NLC publishes some of these in our Fundamental Series. Knowledge and good sense are important factors in passing your exam. Good luck also helps. So now study this Passbook, absorb the material contained within and take that knowledge into the examination. Then do your best to pass that exam.

EXAMINATION SECTION

EXAMINATION SECTION
TEST 1

DIRECTIONS: Each question or incomplete statement is followed by several suggested answers or completions. Select the one that BEST answers the question or completes the statement. *PRINT THE LETTER OF THE CORRECT ANSWER IN THE SPACE AT THE RIGHT.*

1. A specialist is meeting with a panel of local community leaders to determine their perceptions about the effectiveness of a recent outreach program. The leaders seem unresponsive to the specialist's questions, looking at the floor or each other without directly answering the specialist's questions.
One strategy that might work to elicit the desired information would be to
   A. try to discern the hidden meaning of their silence
   B. adopt a mildly confrontational tone and remind them of what's at stake in the community
   C. keep asking open-ended questions and wait patiently for responses
   D. tell them to come back when they're ready to tell you their opinions

1.____

2. Each of the following statements about maintaining a community's attention is true, EXCEPT:
   A. The more challenging it is to pay attention to a message, the more likely it is that it will be attended to
   B. Listeners will be more motivated to pay attention if a speech is personally meaningful
   C. People will be more likely to attend if a speaker pauses to suggest natural transitions in a speech
   D. Listeners will attend to messages that stand out

2.____

3. Each of the following is a key strategy to integrative bargaining among community members in conflict, EXCEPT
   A. focusing on positions, rather than interests
   B. separating the people from the problem
   C. aiming for an outcome based on an objectively identified standard
   D. using active listening skills, such as rephrasing and questioning

3.____

4. Which of the following is NOT one of the major variables to take into account when considering a community needs assessment?
   A. State of program development   B. Resources available
   C. Demographics   D. Community attitudes

4.____

5. Which of the following groups would probably be formed specifically for, or be involved in, the purpose of addressing a specific unmet community need?
   A. An existing consumer group
   B. A council of community representatives
   C. A committee
   D. An existing community organization

5.____

6. If a public outreach campaign designed to mobilize a community fails, the MOST likely reason for this failure is that the campaign
   A. was not specific about what it wanted people to do
   B. was overly serious and did not appeal to people's sense of humor
   C. offered no incentive for the audience to make a change
   D. did not use language that appealed to the audience's emotions

7. Nationwide, the rate of involvement of elderly people in community-based programs demonstrates that they are
   A. under-served when compared to other age groups
   B. served at about the same rate as other age groups
   C. over-served when compared to other age groups
   D. hardly served at all

8. In projecting the likelihood of an education program's success, a domestic violence specialist identifies every single event that must occur to complete the project. The specialist then arranges these events in sequential order and allocates time requirements for each. Finally, the total time is calculated and a model showing all their events and timelines is charted.
   The specialist has used
   A. a PERT chart   B. a simulation
   C. a Markov model   D. the critical path method

9. When working with members of a predominantly African-American community, specialists from other cultural backgrounds should be aware that African-Americans tend to express thoughts and feelings through descriptions of
   A. physically tangible sensations   B. problems to be analyzed
   C. corresponding analogies   D. spiritual issues

10. Local nonprofessionals should be considered useful to a specialist who is looking to undertake a community outreach or educational initiative.
    Which of the following is LEAST likely to be a characteristic or role demonstrated by these community members?
    A. Undertaking support functions at the agency
    B. Serving as a communication channel between the agency and clients
    C. Encouraging greater agency acceptance and credibility within the community
    D. Helping the agency to accomplish meaningful change

11. In working with Native American groups or clients, it is important to recognize that the GREATEST health problem facing their communities today is
    A. domestic violence   B. depression and suicide
    C. alcoholism   D. tuberculosis

12. A specialist is facilitating a cooperative conflict resolution session between community members who have different opinions about what kinds of intervention services should be offered by the local adult protective services agency.
    Which of the following is NOT a guideline that should be followed in this process?
    A. Early in the negotiations, ask each party to name the issues on which they will positively not yield.
    B. Try to get the parties to view the issue from other points of view, beside the two or three conflicting ones.
    C. Have each side volunteer what it would be willing to do to resolve the conflict.
    D. At the end of the session, draw up a formal agreement with agreed-upon actions for both parties.

12.____

13. A specialist wants to evaluate the effectiveness of a local women's shelter. The shelter has suffered from lax participation, given the number of women who have been abused in the surrounding area. The specialist wants to speak with the women in the community who did not follow up on referrals to the shelter, and begins by visiting some of these women. After gaining the trust of these women, the specialist asks for the names of women they know who might be in need of help with a domestic violence situation.
    The specialist's approach in this case is _____ sampling.
    A. maximum variation   B. snowball
    C. convenience   D. typical case

13.____

14. When it comes to perceiving messages, people typically DON'T
    A. tend to simplify causal connections and sometimes even seek a single cause to explain what may be a highly complex effect
    B. tend to perceive messages independently of a categorical framework, especially if the message may be distorted by such an interpretation
    C. have a predisposition toward accepting any pattern that a speaker offers to explain seemingly unconnected facts
    D. tend to interpret things in the way they are viewed by their reference group

14.____

15. The elder members of Native American communities, regardless of kinship, are MOST commonly referred to as
    A. the ancients   B. father or mother
    C. grandfather or grandmother D. chiefs

15.____

16. Each of the following is typically an objective of community mobilization, EXCEPT:
    A. To convince existing community resources to alter their services or work together to address an unmet need
    B. To gather and distribute information to consumers and agencies about unmet needs

16.____

C. To publicize existing community resources and make them more accessible
D. To bring an unmet community need to public attention in order to achieve acceptance of and support for fulfilling the need

17. Research in community outreach shows that women often build friendships through shared positive feelings, whereas men often build friendships through
   A. metacommunication
   B. catharsis
   C. impression management
   D. shared activities

   17._____

18. Typically, the FIRST step in a community-needs assessment is to
   A. identify community's strengths
   B. explore the nature of the neighborhood
   C. get to know the area and its residents
   D. talk to people in the community

   18._____

19. Most public relations experts agree that _____ exposure(s) to a message is the minimum just to get the message noticed. If the aim of a public outreach campaign is action or a change in behavior, the agency budget must plan for more exposures.
   A. one
   B. two
   C. three
   D. four

   19._____

20. In the program development/community liaison model of community work and public outreach, the PRIMARY constituency is considered to be
   A. community representatives and the service agency board or administrators
   B. elected officials, social agencies, and interagency organizations
   C. marginalized or oppressed population groups in a city or region
   D. residents of a neighborhood, parish or rural county

   20._____

21. Social or interpersonal problems in many African-American communities have their roots in
   A. personality deficits
   B. unresolved family conflicts
   C. poor communication
   D. external stressors

   21._____

22. A public outreach campaign should
   I. focus on short-term, measurable goals, rather than ultimate outcomes
   II. try to alter entrenched attitudes within a short time, with powerfully worded messages
   III. proceed in steps or phases, each of which lays out a mechanism that leads to the desired effect
   IV. ignore causes that led to a problem, and instead focus on solutions

   The CORRECT answer is:
   A. I and II
   B. II and III
   C. III only
   D. I, II, III and IV

   22._____

23. Research findings indicate that in listing preferences for helping professional attributes, individuals from culturally diverse groups are MOST likely to consider _____ as more important than _____.
    A. personality similarity; either race/ethnic similarity or attitude similarity
    B. therapist experience; any kind of similarity
    C. race/ethnic similarity; attitude similarity
    D. attitude similarity; race/ethnic similarity

24. Each of the following is considered to be an objective of community organization EXCEPT
    A. effecting changes in the distribution of decision-making power
    B. helping people develop and strengthen the traits of self-direction and cooperation
    C. effecting and maintaining the balance between needs and resources in a community
    D. helping people deal with their problems by developing alternative behaviors

25. A specialist is helping the adult protective services agency to design a public outreach campaign. The topic to be addressed is complex, public understanding is low, and most professionals at the agency feel that having more complete information might change the opinions of community members. Which method of pre-campaign research is probably MOST appropriate?
    A. Deliberative polling
    B. Attitude scales
    C. Surveys or questionnaires
    D. Focus groups

KEY (CORRECT ANSWERS)

1.	C		11.	C
2.	A		12.	A
3.	A		13.	B
4.	C		14.	B
5.	C		15.	C
6.	A		16.	B
7.	A		17.	D
8.	D		18.	B
9.	C		19.	C
10.	A		20.	A

21.	D
22.	C
23.	D
24.	D
25.	A

TEST 2

DIRECTIONS: Each question or incomplete statement is followed by several suggested answers or completions. Select the one that BEST answers the question or completes the statement. *PRINT THE LETTER OF THE CORRECT ANSWER IN THE SPACE AT THE RIGHT.*

1. A specialist has been called in to resolve a dispute between two community leaders who have been arguing about the level of service needed within the community. The discussion has been going on for several hours when the specialist arrives, and both people seem to be upset.
   After calming the two down and getting each of them to agree on a statement of the problem, the specialist should ask each person to
   A. summarize his or her argument in three main points
   B. explain why he or she became so upset
   C. clearly state, in objective terms, the position of the other in a form that meets with the other's approval
   D. identify the best alternative outcome, other than their presumed ideal

   1._____

2. In evaluating the impact of a public outreach campaign, the _____ model can be used early in the campaign to address first impressions.
   A. exposure or advertising
   B. expert interview
   C. impact monitoring or process
   D. experimental or quasi-experimental

   2._____

3. When trying to motivate an older population to take action on a community problem, it is helpful to remember that older people
   A. are more self-reliant in their decision-making than other members of the same family
   B. often need more time to decide than younger people
   C. are more likely than younger people to view community problems self-referentially
   D. tend to take a pragmatic, rather than philosophical, view of life

   3._____

4. The method of group or community decision-making that is normally MOST time-consuming is
   A. majority opinion   B. consensus
   C. expert opinion   D. authority rule

   4._____

5. A local adult protective services agency has identified one of the goals of its recent public outreach campaign to be the mobilization of activists.
   The campaign should probably
   A. target neutral audiences
   B. home in on supporters
   C. stick to purely factual information
   D. try to persuade community fence-sitters

   5._____

6. Research of Native American youths' perceptions of family concerns for their well-being has generally found that these youths
   A. have a high degree of uncertainty about their families' feelings toward them
   B. believe their families don't care about them
   C. believe that their mothers care a great deal about them, but their fathers don't
   D. believe their families care a great deal about them

7. A domestic violence specialist is developing a new outreach program for the local community. The specialist has defined the target problem, set program goals, and planned the actions that will take place as a result of the program. Most likely, the next step will be to
   A. evaluate the resources available to achieve program goals
   B. define and sequence the steps that will be taken to achieve program goals
   C. determine how the program will be evaluated
   D. decide how the program will operate

8. Elder: *I'm so glad to have someone to talk to, someone who really understands my problem.*
   Specialist: *It is nice to be able to talk to someone who will listen.*
   Elder: *That's for sure.*
   In the above exchange, what listening skill is evident in the underlined statement?
   A. Verbatim response
   B. Paraphrasing
   C. Advising
   D. Evaluation

9. Which of the following activities is involved in the specialist's task of mobilizing?
   A. Meeting individuals in the community with problems and assisting them in finding help
   B. Identifying unmet community needs
   C. Speaking out against an unjust policy or procedure
   D. Developing new services or linking presently available services to meet community needs

10. The preliminary research associated with a public outreach campaign should FIRST be aimed at determining
    A. the budget
    B. the message's ultimate audience
    C. what media to use
    D. the short-term behavioral goals of the campaign

11. A specialist in a low-income community wants to plan programs that will deal with the influence of unemployment on domestic disturbances. The specialist needs to know not only how many unemployed people are in the community now, but also how many people will be unemployed at any particular tie in the future, and how those numbers will vary given certain conditions.

Probably the BEST way to trace employment rates over time and within differing conditions is through the use of
A. the critical path
B. linear programming
C. difference equations
D. the Markov model

12. Generally, public outreach programs—whatever their stated goal—should
    I. create a sense of urgency about a problem
    II. decline to identify opponents of the issue or idea
    III. propose concrete, easily understandable solutions
    IV. urge a specific action

    The CORRECT answer is:
    A. I only
    B. I, III and IV
    C. II and III
    D. I, II, III and IV

13. Which of the following methods of community needs assessment relies to the GREATEST degree on existing public records?
    A. Social indicators
    B. Field study
    C. Rates under treatment
    D. Key informant

14. During an interview with a Native American client, a specialist is careful to maintain close and nearly constant eye contact.
    The client is MOST likely to interpret this as a(n)
    A. show of high concern
    B. sign of disrespect
    C. uncomfortable assumption of intimacy
    D. attempt to intimidate

15. The BEST strategy for addressing an audience that is known to be captive, or even hostile, is to
    A. refer to experiences in common
    B. flatter the audience
    C. joke about things in or near the audience
    D. plead for fairness

16. Integrative conflict resolution is characterized by
    A. an overriding concern to maximize joint outcomes
    B. one side's interests opposing the other's
    C. a fixed and limited amount of resources to be divided, so that the more one group gets, the less another gets
    D. manipulation and withholding information as negotiation strategies

17. A specialist wants to learn how to interact with the members of a largely Latino community in a more culturally sensitive way.
    Which of the following is NOT a guideline for interacting with members of a Latino community?
    A. Efforts to foster independence and self-reliance may be interpreted by many Latinos as a lack of concern for others.
    B. Efforts to deal one-on-one with an adolescent client may serve to alienate the parents, especially the mother.

C. A nonverbal gesture, such as lowering the eyes, is interpreted by many Latinos as a sign of respect and deference to authority.
D. In much of Latino culture, the focus of control for problems tends to be much more external than internal.

18. Each of the following is a supporting assumption of community organization, EXCEPT:
    A. Democracy requires cooperative participation.
    B. In order for communities to change, it is necessary for each individual in the community to be willing to change.
    C. Communities often need help with organization and planning.
    D. Holistic approaches work better than fragmented or ad-hoc programs.

19. Helping professionals often have difficulty to bring community resources together to fulfill unmet community needs.
    Which of the following is NOT usually a reason for this?
    A. Some community groups resist assistance when it is offered.
    B. Few community groups make their needs known.
    C. Community resources frequently change the type of services they offer.
    D. Often, community resources prefer to work alone.

20. When dealing with groups or populations of elderly clients, specialists should be mindful that about _____ of the nation's elderly suffer from mental health problems.
    A. a tenth   B. a quarter   C. a third   D. half

21. In an African-American community, a specialist from another culture should recognize that church participation, for most African-Americans, is viewed as a
    A. method for maintaining control and communicating competency
    B. way of depersonalizing problems or troubles
    C. way to divert attention away from problems
    D. means of cathartic emotional release

22. Adult protective service programs supported by state statutes protect elderly people from abuse and neglect under the doctrine of
    A. parens patriae   B. habeas corpus
    C. in loco parentis   D. volenti non fit injuria

23. In terms of public outreach, which of the following statements about an audience is NOT generally true?
    A. The more heterogeneous the audience, the more necessary it will be to use specific examples and appeals to certain types of people.
    B. The smaller the audience, the more likely that its members will share assumptions and values.
    C. When the speaker does not know the status of an audience, it is best to assume that they are captive rather than voluntary.
    D. The larger an audience, the more formal a presentation is likely to be.

24. A specialist often spends time in the places frequented by community residents. She listens carefully to what residents seem most concerned about, and engages many in conversations, asking them how they see the problems in the community. During these conversations, she makes mental notes about whether the statements of the problems are the same things that are mentioned in their conversations. From these conversations, the worker determines what she thinks the unmet needs of the community are.
Which of the key issues in identifying unmet needs has the worker neglected to address?
    A. The different points of view regarding the issues, and whether there is any common ground
    B. Whether the stated problems and conversations with community residents reflect the same concerns
    C. How community residents define the issues
    D. What the residents talk about with one another in a community

25. Which of the following political styles should be used to promote an issue that could become controversial if it is perceived to involve major reforms?
    A. High-conflict, polarized
    B. High-conflict, consensual
    C. Moderate conflict, compromise-oriented
    D. Low-conflict, technical

KEY (CORRECT ANSWERS)

1.	C		11.	D
2.	A		12.	B
3.	B		13.	A
4.	B		14.	B
5.	B		15.	A
6.	D		16.	A
7.	A		17.	D
8.	B		18.	B
9.	D		19.	C
10.	B		20.	B

21. D
22. A
23. A
24. A
25. D

EXAMINATION SECTION
TEST 1

DIRECTIONS: Each question or incomplete statement is followed by several suggested answers or completions. Select the one that BEST answers the question or completes the statement. *PRINT THE LETTER OF THE CORRECT ANSWER IN THE SPACE AT THE RIGHT.*

Questions 1-10.

DIRECTIONS: For each of the sentences given below, numbered 1 through 10, select from the following choices the MOST correct choice and print your choice in the space at the right. Select as your answer:
- A – if the statement contains an unnecessary word of expression
- B – if the statement contains a slang term or expression ordinarily not acceptable in government report writing
- C – if the statement contains an old-fashioned word or expression, where a concrete, plain term would be more useful
- D – if the statement contains no major faults

1. Every one of us should try harder.   1.____
2. Yours of the first instant has been received.   2.____
3. We will have to do a real snow job on him.   3.____
4. I shall contact him next Thursday.   4.____
5. None of us were invited to the meeting with the community.   5.____
6. We got this here job to do.   6.____
7. She could not help but see the mistake in the checkbook.   7.____
8. Don't bug the Director about the report.   8.____
9. I beg to inform you that your letter has been received.   9.____
10. This project is all screwed up.   10.____

Questions 11-15.

DIRECTIONS: Read the following Inter-office Memo. Then answer Questions 11 through 15 based ONLY on the memo.

INTER-OFFICE MEMORANDUM

To: Alma Robinson, Human Resources Aide
From: Frank Shields, Social Worker

I would like to have you help Mr. Edward Tunney who is trying to raise his two children by himself. He needs to learn to improve the physical care of his children and especially of his daughter Helen, age 9. She is avoided and ridiculed at school because her hair is uncombed, her teeth not properly cleaned, her clothing torn, wrinkled and dirty, as well as shabby and poorly fitted. The teachers and school officials have contacted the Department and the social worker for two years about Helen. She is not able to make friends because of these problems. I have talked to Mr. Tunney about improvements for the child's clothing, hair, and hygiene. He tends to deny these things are problems, but is cooperative, and a second person showing him the importance of better physical care for Helen would be helpful.

Perhaps you could teach Helen how to fix her own hair. She has all the materials. I would also like you to form your own opinion of the sanitary conditions in the home and how they could be improved.

Mr. Tunney is expecting your visit and is willing to talk with you about ways he can help with these problems.

11. In the above memorandum, the Human Resources Aide is being asked to help Mr. Tunney to

   A. improve the learning habits of his children
   B. enable his children to make friends at school
   C. take responsibility for the upbringing of his children
   D. give attention to the grooming and cleanliness of his children

12. This case was brought to the attention of the social worker by

   A. government officials
   B. teachers and school officials
   C. the Department
   D. Mr. Tunney

13. In general, Mr. Tunney's attitude with regard to his children could BEST be described as

   A. interested in correcting the obvious problems, but unable to do so alone
   B. unwilling to follow the advice of those who are trying to help
   C. concerned, but unaware of the seriousness of these problems
   D. interested in helping them, but afraid of taking the advice of the social worker

14. Which of the following actions has NOT been suggested as a possible step for the Human Resources Aide to take?

   A. Help Helen to learn to care for herself by teaching her grooming skills
   B. Determine ways of improvement through information gathered on a home visit
   C. Discuss her own views on Helen's problems with school officials
   D. Ask Mr. Tunney in what ways he believes the physical care may be improved

15. According to the memo, the Human Resources Aide is ESPECIALLY being asked to observe and form her own opinions about   15._____

    A. the relationship between Mr. Tunney and the school officials
    B. Helen's attitude toward her classmates and teacher
    C. the sanitary conditions in the home
    D. the reasons Mr. Tunney is not cooperative with the agency

16. In one day, an aide receives 18 inquiries by phone and 27 inquiries in person. What percentage of the inquiries received that day were by phone?   16._____

    A. 33%   B. 40%   C. 45%   D. 60%

17. If the weekly pay checks for 5 part-time employees are: $129.32, $162.74, $143.67, $135.75, and $156.56, then the combined weekly income for the 5 employees is   17._____

    A. $727.84   B. $728.04   C. $730.84   D. $737.04

18. Suppose that there are 17 aides working in an office where many community complaints are received by telephone. In one ten-day period, 4250 calls were received. If the same number of calls were received each day, and the aides divided the work load equally, about how many calls did each aide respond to daily?   18._____

    A. 25   B. 35   C. 75   D. 250

19. Suppose that an assignment was divided among 5 aides. If the first aide spent 67 hours on the assignment, the second aide spent 95 hours, the third aide spent 52 hours, the fourth aide spent 78 hours, and the fifth aide spent 103 hours, what was the AVERAGE amount of time spent by each aide on the assignment?   19._____
    _____ hours.

    A. 71   B. 75   C. 79   D. 83

20. If there are 240 employees in a center and 1/3 are absent on the day of a bad snowstorm, how many employees were at work in the center on that day?   20._____

    A. 80   B. 120   C. 160   D. 200

KEY (CORRECT ANSWERS)

1. D
2. C
3. B
4. D
5. D

6. B
7. D
8. B
9. C
10. B

11. D
12. B
13. C
14. C
15. C

16. B
17. B
18. A
19. C
20. C

TEST 2

DIRECTIONS: Each question or incomplete statement is followed by several suggested answers or completions. Select the one that BEST answers the question or completes the statement. *PRINT THE LETTER OF THE CORRECT ANSWER IN THE SPACE AT THE RIGHT.*

1. Suppose that an aide takes 25 minutes to prepare a letter to a client. 1._____
   If the aide is assigned to prepare 9 letters on a certain day, how much time should she set aside for this task? _____ hours.

   A. 3 3/4   B. 4 1/4   C. 4 3/4   D. 5 1/4

2. Suppose that a certain center uses both Form A and Form B in the course of its daily 2._____
   work, and that Form A is used 4 times as often as Form B.
   If the total number of both forms used in one week is 750, how many times was Form A used?

   A. 100   B. 200   C. 400   D. 600

3. Suppose a center has a budget of $1092.70 from which 8 desks costing $78.05 apiece 3._____
   must be bought?
   How many ADDITIONAL desks can be ordered from this budget after the 8 desks have been purchased?

   A. 4   B. 6   C. 9   D. 14

4. When researching a particular case, a team of 16 aides was asked to check through 234 4._____
   folders to obtain the necessary information.
   If half the aides worked twice as fast as the other half, and the slow group checked through 12 folders each hour, about how long would it take to complete the assignment? _____ hours.

   A. $4\frac{1}{4}$ B. 5   C. 6   D. $6\frac{1}{2}$

5. The difference in the cost of two printers is $28.32. If the less expensive printer 5._____
   costs $153.61, what is the cost of the other printer?

   A. $171.93   B. $172.03   C. $181.93   D. $182.03

Questions 6-8.

DIRECTIONS: Questions 6 through 8 are to be answered on the basis of the following information contained on a sample page of a payroll book.

Emp. No.	Name of Employee	Hours Worked M	T	W	Th	F	Total Hours Worked	Pay PerHour	Total Wages
1	James Smith	8	8	8	8	8			$480.00
2	Gloria Jones	8	7 3/4	7		7 1/2		$16.00	$560.00
3	Robert Adams	6	6	7 1/2	7 1/2	8 3/4		$18.28	

6. The pay per hour of Employee No. 1 is   6.____
   A. $12.00   B. $13.72   C. $15.00   D. $19.20

7. The number of hours that Employee No. 2 worked on Friday is   7.____
   A. 4   B. 5 1/2   C. 4.63   D. 4 3/4

8. The total wages for Employee No. 3 is   8.____
   A. $636.92   B. $648.94   C. $661.04   D. $672.96

9. As a rule, the FIRST step in writing a check should be to   9.____
   A. number the check
   B. write in the payee's name
   C. tear out the check stub
   D. write the purpose of the check in the space provided at the bottom

10. If an error is made when writing a check, the MOST widely accepted procedure is to   10.____
    A. draw a line through the error and initial it
    B. destroy both the check and check stub by tearing into small pieces
    C. erase the error if it does not occur in the amount of the check
    D. write *Void* across both the check and check stub and save them

11. The check that is MOST easily cashed is one that is   11.____
    A. not signed   B. made payable to *Cash*
    C. post-dated   D. endorsed in part

12.   12.____

No. *103*	$ *142. 77*
May 14	
To *Alan Jacobs*	
For *Wages (5/6-5/10)*	
Bal. Bro't For 'd	2340. 63
Amt. Deposited	205. 24
Total	
Amt. This Check	142. 77
Bal. Car'd For 'd	

The balance to be carried forward on the check stub above is
A. $2,278.16   B. $1,992.62   C. $2,688.64   D. $2,403.10

13. The procedure for reconciling a bank statement consists of _____ the bank balance   13.____
    and _____ the checkbook balance.

    A. *adding* outstanding checks to; *subtracting* the service and check charges from
    B. *subtracting* the service charge from; *subtracting* outstanding checks from
    C. *subtracting* the service charge from; *adding* outstanding checks to
    D. *subtracting* outstanding checks from; *subtracting* the service and check charges from

14. An employee makes $15.70 an hour and receives time-and-a-half in overtime pay for every hour more than 40 in a given week. If the employee works 47 hours, the employee's total wages for that week would be

    A. $792.85   B. $837.90   C. $875.25   D. $1,106.85

15. A high-speed copier can make 25,000 copies before periodic service is required. Before this service is necessary, _____ copies of a 137-page document can be printed.

    A. 211   B. 204   C. 190   D. 178

16. An aide is typing a letter to the James Weldon Johnson Head Start Center. To be sure that a Mr. Joseph Maxwell reads it, an attention line is typed below the inside address. The salutation should, therefore, read:

    A. To Whom It May Concern: B. Dear Mr. Maxwell:
    C. Gentlemen: D. Dear Joseph:

17. When describing the advantages of the numeric filing system, it is NOT true that it

    A. is the most accurate of all methods
    B. allows for unlimited expansion according to the needs of the agency
    C. is a system useful for filing letters directly according to name or subject
    D. allows for cross-referencing

18. In writing a letter for your Center, the PURPOSE of the letter should usually be stated in

    A. the first paragraph. This assists the reader in making more sense of the letter.
    B. the second paragraph. The first paragraph should be used to confirm receipt of the letter being answered
    C. the last paragraph. The first paragraphs should be used to build up to the purpose of the letter.
    D. any paragraph. Each letter has a different purpose and the letter should conform to that purpose.

19. If you open a personal letter addressed to another aide by mistake, the one of the following actions which it would generally be BEST for you to take is to

    A. reseal the envelope or place the contents in another envelope and pass it on to the employee
    B. place the letter inside the envelope, indicate under your initials that it was opened in error and give it to the employee
    C. personally give the employee the letter without any explanation
    D. ignore your error, attach the envelope to the letter, and give it out in the usual manner

20. Of the following, the MAIN purpose of the head start program is to

    A. provide programs for pre-school development of children
    B. provide children between the ages of 6 and 12 with after-school activity
    C. establish a system for providing care for teenage youngsters with working parents
    D. supervise centers providing 24-hour child care

KEY (CORRECT ANSWERS)

1. A
2. D
3. B
4. D
5. C

6. A
7. D
8. B
9. A
10. D

11. B
12. D
13. D
14. A
15. D

16. C
17. C
18. A
19. B
20. A

EXAMINATION SECTION
TEST 1

DIRECTIONS: Each question or incomplete statement is followed by several suggested answers or completions. Select the one that BEST answers the question or completes the statement. *PRINT THE LETTER OF THE CORRECT ANSWER IN THE SPACE AT THE RIGHT.*

1. One day an elderly man asks you if he can apply for Social Security at the welfare office.
   Your response should be to
   A. tell him that it is foolish to think he can apply for Social Security at the welfare office
   B. take him back to his apartment because he is too old to be roaming the streets asking questions
   C. explain that Social Security is a federal program and direct him to the nearest Social Security office
   D. call his daughter and tell her that the family should take better care of their father

   1.____

2. One of your duties is to occasionally visit clients. On one occasion, you visit Mrs. B., who needs assistance in referral of her children for day care so that she may enter a job training program. She has postponed completing the referral.
   What should you do in this situation?
   A. Tell her that if she doesn't hurry there will be no room at the day care center and the training program will be closed
   B. Make the arrangements and tell Mrs. B. that she should do what you say
   C. Remember that all people who ask for help are not always ready to receive it and continue to allow Mrs. B. to complete the referral by herself
   D. The next time Mrs. B. asks for help, see that she gets it as slowly as possible

   2.____

3. Assume that you are trying to contact a community group to offer to meet with their representative to explain a new agency policy about intake procedures.
   In order to "get your message across," you should
   A. write a short concise letter explaining why you want to meet with them and when you will be available
   B. write a short letter stating only that it is important that they contact you in order to arrange a meeting
   C. ask a secretary to help you because you do not really like to write to groups
   D. call the agency rather than write since you know someone there

   3.____

4. It is necessary for you to call the director of a head start center in order to discuss   4._____
a training program for teaching aides. The operator asks who you are and
what you wish to discuss with the director.
Your response should be to
   A. tell her that you would rather explain to the director and you want to
      speak to her immediately
   B. identify yourself, your department, and the nature of your business with
      the director
   C. hang up and try to call again when another operator is on duty
   D. tell your supervisor that the operator at the head start center is rude and
      you would rather not be asked to call there again

5. Mr. A. wants her children to go to summer camp. She has receive the request   5._____
forms, but does not understand all of the questions and you are asked to help
her complete them. She comes to the office at the appointed time.
Of the following, the action you should take is to
   A. tell her she has taken so long that maybe the children will not go to camp
   B. see her as quickly as possible, explain the questions to her, and help her
      in completing the forms
   C. help her, but tell her she will have to learn to read better and refer her to
      an evening school
   D. fill out the forms or her by yourself

6. Mrs. B. needs a referral to the cancer clinic. You contact the clinic and make   6._____
arrangements for her visit. You go to her home to inform her about the time
because she has no phone. She thanks you for your help and then offers you
a piece of jewelry that appears to be rather expensive.
Of the following, the action you should take is to
   A. take the gift because you don't want to hurt her feelings
   B. tell her that she is foolish and should spend her money on herself
   C. explain to her that you are pleased with her thoughtfulness, but you are
      unable to accept the gift
   D. refuse the gift and get someone else to make referrals in the future
      because she is trying to pay you for your help

7. Mrs. C., a seemingly healthy, intelligent woman whose husband is disabled, and   7._____
who works part-time, asks for help in getting homemaker services.
Of the following, the action you should take is to
   A. give Mrs. C. the necessary information and help her get the services
   B. tell Mrs. C. that you do not feel she needs these services since her
      husband is capable of helping
   C. make note of her request since you do not feel it is urgent
   D. refer her to a caseworker since she obviously needs help in defining her
      role as a woman

8. When you are interviewing clients, it is important to notice and record how they   8._____
say what they say—angrily, nervously, or with "body English" —because these
signs may

A. tell you that the client's words are the opposite of what the client feels and you may need to dig to find out what those feelings are
B. be the prelude to violent behavior which no aide is prepared to handle
C. show that the client does not really deserve serious consideration
D. be important later should you be asked to defend what you did for the client

9. You are recording a visit you have made with a client who was angry and abusive to you during the interview. At one point, you lost your temper and said some things that you immediately regretted. You are embarrassed to record that you lost your temper.
However, it would be desirable to record this MAINLY because
A. you would feel guilty if you did not record it
B. your supervisor might hear about it from the client, so it would be better to have it written down from your point of view
C. your supervisor can use the information to help you to improve your skills
D. it is agency policy to write down everything

10. Through one of your clients you learn that a day care program's hours have been extended. You confirm this information with the day care center.
It is then MOST important for you to
A. make a note of this fact, since it will mean you have to change your schedule in working with the client
B. add this information to your personal resource file so that you can refer other clients to the day dare program
C. inform your supervisor of the new information so that it can be added to the central resource file
D. ignore the information, since your client does not need to have her child in day care for any extra hours

11. You are sent to a meeting of day-care parents to explain the programs of your agency. One of the parents becomes very angry, saying that welfare departments treat people like animals.
You should remain as calm as possible and say to the parent that
A. he is right, but you have no control over what your agency does
B. he is disrupting the meeting and you have come to explain a program, not to listen to complaints
C. you understand his feelings and that sometimes clients do not get the services they wish as quickly as possible; however, you will do whatever you can to assist him
D. he should call your supervisor tomorrow and make an appointment to discuss his feelings

12. Assume that you receive a telephone call from a very angry father. His daughter took money from his wallet, and he wants the caseworker to control the daughter. He yells, screams, and swears at you.
What is the BEST way for you to respond?

A. Hang up because you are not responsible for his daughter's actions. He shouldn't scream and swear at you.
B. Remember to be courteous and polite at all times, never losing your temper
C. Transfer the call to the supervisor because you are concerned about the father's unreasonableness and do not want the responsibility of dealing with him
D. Tell him that behavior such as he is demonstrating is the reason his daughter steals from him

13. Mrs. D.'s son, aged 12, has been getting into difficulty in the neighborhood. At a community meeting, she asks your help in finding worthwhile activities for him. It is APPROPRIATE for you to respond to her because
    A. you should have knowledge of the social services available in the neighborhood and the activities they offer
    B. you have known Mrs. D. and her family for several years and know how much trouble she has had with her son
    C. it is your job to do what the caseworker assigns to you without question
    D. you are concerned about impressing Mrs. D with your knowledge

14. Several clients live in your neighborhood. They know that you work for the human resources administration. One day one of them tells you that there is a rumor that another client is pregnant and asks if this is true. You know from a past discussion with the caseworker that this client is pregnant.
    The BEST answer for you to give would be to
    A. tell her it is none of her business and if she wants to know, she should ask the caseworker
    B. ask her who told her that this client is pregnant
    C. explain that anything told to the agency is held in confidence and will not be shared with anyone else
    D. tell her you don't know, but will ask when you get back to the office and let her know later

15. The area senior citizens group asks for an agency representative to discuss old-age assistance and new SSI regulations. Your supervisor asks you to attend this meeting; however, you do not wish to go because you really do not feel that you work well with older people. In fact, you don't like them very much.
    What should be your response?
    A. Tell the supervisor that you cannot go because you have an appointment with the doctor that day
    B. Get another worker to go for you and assume his task while he is gone
    C. Explain to your supervisor what problems you have in working with old-age clients
    D. Go, because you should do the tasks that are assigned to you according to your job description

16. At a center where you are distributing literature about agency programs, a citizen comes up to you and begins to complain loudly about agency programs. What should be your response?
    A. Call the police and have the complainer removed from the center
    B. Tell him that you do not make policy; suggest that he go to the office and complain
    C. Remain as calm as possible and ask that he discuss the complaints with you calmly. If necessary, make an appointment with him
    D. Yell at him since this seems to be the way he relates to agency people

17. A community group is having a training program. You are sent to explain agency policy and answer questions.
    Providing this type of contact between the agency and community groups is PROPER because
    A. you like people and are a good public speaker
    B. it is the responsibility of the agency to cooperate with community groups in order to help the public to be well-informed about agency policy
    C. you were once in the same training program and understand the kind of people who are being trained
    D. once in a while everyone should have the opportunity to speak to a community group

18. While you are assisting in the intake area, a young man who is applying is cooperative but begins to ask you personal questions: your age, where you live, whether you have children, and other similar questions.
    You are disturbed by these questions, so you should
    A. tell him that agency policy does not allow you to answer personal questions and send him to another intake worker
    B. tell him it is your responsibility to ask questions, not his
    C. tell your supervisor that you do not want to work in intake because clients can get too nosy and you get nervous
    D. avoid answering personal questions and try to get him to return to the purpose of the interview

19. You are assigned to the reception area for the day. A mother arrives in the office with three small children. In a rage, she says that she does not have enough money to feed the children and demands that you find a home for them.
    The BEST action for you to take should be to
    A. call a security officer and have him remove her and the children from the office
    B. attempt to calm her down by listening to her, attend to the children's needs and call for a supervisor
    C. take the children from her and ask her to leave at once
    D. call the supervisor and security because it is their job to take care of abusive clients

20. Assume that you are interviewing a young unwed mother who has recently arrived in the city from Alabama. She is a likable girl and is very cooperative. However, it is difficult to understand the meaning of her conversation due to her accent and different use of words.
You would like to establish a good relationship with her, so you should FIRST
   A. suggest that she go to evening school so that she can learn to speak like other people in the city
   B. tell her that you don't understand her sometimes and you would appreciate it if she would explain what she means
   C. take another worker with you on visits to help you in the interview
   D. try to find a worker in the agency who has a similar background and have the case handled by the worker

21. A man being interviewed is entitled to Medicaid, but he refuses to sign up for it because he says he cannot accept any form of welfare.
Of the following, the BEST course of action for an aide to take FIRST is to
   A. try to discover the reason for his feeling this way
   B. tell him that he should be glad financial help is available
   C. explain that others cannot get help him if he will not help himself
   D. suggest that he speak to someone who is already on Medicaid

22. Of the following, the outcome of an interview by an aide depends MOS heavily on the
   A. personality of the interviewee
   B. personality of the aide
   C. subject matter of the questions asked
   D. interaction between aide and interviewee

23. Some patients being interviewed are PRIMARILY interested in making a favorable impression. The aide should be aware of the fact that such patients are more likely than other patients to
   A. try to anticipate the answers the interviewer is looking for
   B. answer all questions openly and frankly
   C. try to assume the role of interviewer
   D. be anxious to get the interview over as quickly as possible

24. The type of interview which an aide usually conducts is substantially different from most interviewing situations in all of the following aspects EXCEPT the
   A. setting   B. kinds of clients
   C. techniques employed   D. kinds of problems

25. During an interview, an aide uses a "leading question."
This type of question is so-called because it generally
   A. starts a series of questions about one topic
   B. suggests the answer which the aide wants
   C. forms the basis for a following "trick" question
   D. sets, at the beginning, the tone of the interview

KEY (CORRECT ANSWERS)

1.	C		11.	C
2.	C		12.	B
3.	A		13.	A
4.	B		14.	C
5.	B		15.	C
6.	C		16.	C
7.	A		17.	B
8.	A		18.	D
9.	C		19.	B
10.	C		20.	B

21. A
22. D
23. A
24. C
25. B

TEST 2

DIRECTIONS: Each question or incomplete statement is followed by several suggested answers or completions. Select the one that BEST answers the question or completes the statement. *PRINT THE LETTER OF THE CORRECT ANSWER IN THE SPACE AT THE RIGHT.*

1. Miss Lally is an old-age assistance recipient. Her health is not good and it is important that she have three good meals each day. She follows these instructions except on Friday she refuses to eat meat because of her religious beliefs. She will not even substitute fish.
   You are very concerned about this, so you should
   A. tell your supervisor so that she will go to see Miss Lally and make her eat nourishing meals on Friday
   B. call her doctor and tell him so that he will see her and explain to her that fasting is not good for her health
   C. attempt to understand her value system and accept that it is possible that she is acting in good faith with her own values even though they may be harmful to her health
   D. explain to her how important it is that she eat meat each day in order to be in good health and enjoy the remaining years of her life

2. Theodore is a junkie. Every cent he can get his hands on legally or illegally is used to supply his habit. You are angry because the junkie is destroying himself and his family. You feel that the courts should punish him for his illegal acts.
   Of the following, the BEST action for you to take is to
   A. suggest to your supervisor that the income maintenance center reduce the family grant, taking out his portion
   B. help his wife to find another apartment for her and the children away from him
   C. call the local police to find out why they are doing nothing about this man's activities in the community
   D. reconsider your ideas about punishment, remembering that punishment alone will not help the man to change his behavior

3. You are regularly assigned to taking Sarah Jones and her young son to the clinic. She is a very warm, friendly woman and your relationship with her is good. However, she invited you to come for dinner on Sunday and to go to a school play with her. You would like to accept the invitations because you need weekend activities and you like her.
   What should be your PRIMARY consideration in coming to a decision?
   A. You need friends just as she does, so you should accept the invitations
   B. You are a worker and should not be seen with a client in public places
   C. Decide whether accepting the invitations will help to meet agency needs or will hamper the relationship you are expected to establish
   D. Tell her "no" because it is not a good policy to be on such friendly terms with clients

4. Martha's husband has been arrested in a drug raid and she is extremely anxious. Your supervisor asks that you visit her to determine ways in which the agency may help her. You visit and find her weeping; the house and the children have obviously been neglected.
The BEST thing for you to do is to
   A. tell her to stop crying and help her to clean the apartment and the children
   B. remind her that her husband has been warned and now has to pay for not listening
   C. listen to her, allowing her to express her feelings of fear, loss, and grief, and reassure her of your concern
   D. listen to her but caution her that she is neglecting the home and children because of her anxiety and you may have to ask your supervisor to remove the children if she doesn't get any better

4.____

5. Mrs. Dwight's landlord is very slow in making repairs in her apartment. Each time you see her, she complains about this over and over again, calling her landlord names and threatening to report him to the city. She complains to any agency person she meets.
Realizing that these complaints are not getting any action, you should
   A. avoid meeting with her because she is annoying
   B. suggest that she see a doctor because she is irrational and should get some help
   C. ask her what she would like to do about the problem and assist her in carrying out her plans
   D. ask the supervisor to see her because you do not have the skills to help her

5.____

6. In the day-to-day operations of the human resources administration, which of the following would you consider to be the PRIMARY function of the agency?
   A. Getting work done to meet city and federal deadlines
   B. Being sure that all of the clients who come to the agency are seen before closing time
   C. Delivering services to those persons who are eligible for assistance
   D. Making sure everyone gets his check on time

6.____

7. During the course of an interview you find it is necessary to arrange a special appointment for the client to return for a further interview. After checking your calendar, you tell the client the date she is to come back. The client, however, says she cannot see you on that date because she is to attend a rally at a community center in her neighborhood.
Of the following, your BEST action should be to
   A. let her know that any other day is an inconvenience to you and remind her that the appointment is for her benefit
   B. forget about the special appointment and try to get along with the information you have
   C. explain to her the need for the appointment and ask when she can meet with you
   D. tell her that since the community center is not city-operated, she must keep her appointment with you

7.____

8. In working with community groups, it is important that you be able to define what a community is.
Of the following definitions, which is the MOST appropriate?
A community
   A. consists of a group of people living fairly close together in a more or less compact territory, who come together in their chief concerns
   B. is a particular section of a city designated on a census tract
   C. is that portion of a city which constitutes an election district
   D. is a section of a city or town in which a particular ethnic group conducts its social, business, and religious life

8.____

9. The agency has implemented a new policy regarding the intake procedure. You wish to explain and discuss this policy with as many community groups as possible. You make an initial contact by mail.
In order to get your message across well, your letter should be
   A. short and as concise as possible explaining why you want to meet with them, and offer several possible times that you will be available
   B. short, explaining only that it is important that the groups contact you in order to arrange a meeting
   C. drafted by the center's secretary and sent to the usual groups
   D put in the usual announcement form in the center's newsletter

9.____

10. A group of young welfare mothers want to form an organization that will provide babysitting services for mothers of children who are too young to enroll in a day care center.
What should be your answer to them?
   A. Tell them to try to get the center to change its policy to include young children
   B. Arrange the time to meet with them to offer as much advice and support as possible, since most communities do need this service
   C. Suggest that it may be better that they spend their time taking care of their own children
   D. Ask a social worker to survey the community to determine if such a service is really needed at this time

10.____

11. New regulations have removed the disabled, blind, and old-age assistance cases from the public assistance caseload. Assistance in these categories is given directly by the federal government. A former client has not received his check. The chairman of the senior citizens committee calls and angrily demands that your agency do something in this man's behalf.
In response, you should
   A. answer politely, explaining that your agency is not concerned about OAA clients
   B. arrange to meet with him in order to discuss the new policy
   C. refer him to the Social Security office covering the area where the client lives
   D. ask that he call again when he is calmer so that you may discuss this matter with him

11.____

12. A high school student from the community comes to see you about a homework assignment to write a report on your center.
    The BEST way to help him is to
    A. refer him to a social worker who has daily contact with clients in their homes
    B. contact the boy's teacher and find out why you were not warned of his coming
    C. explain your center's program and answer as many of his questions as you can
    D. give him literature about the welfare system in the city and state

13. Assume that the women's group of the Community Baptist Church has invited you to a Sunday afternoon service to celebrate the tenth anniversary of the pastor. The agency's relationship with the women is good in that they often offer their homes as emergency homes for adult clients.
    What should you do about the invitation?
    A. Do not attend but send them a note congratulating the pastor and explaining that agency personnel do not work on Sundays
    B. Ask a social worker who lives close to the church to go
    C. Accept the invitation if at all possible, attend the service and whatever social hour they may have afterwards
    D. Ignore the invitation since this function has little relationship to your job

14. Suppose that a person you are interviewing becomes angry at some of the questions you have asked, calls you meddlesome and nosy, and states that she will not answer those questions.
    Of the following, which is the BEST action for you to take
    A. Explain the reasons the questions are asked and the importance of the answers
    B. Inform the interviewee that you are only doing your job and advise her that she should answer your questions or leave your office
    C. Report to your supervisor what the interviewee called you and refuse to continue the interview
    D. End the interview and tell the interviewee she will not be serviced by your department

15. Suppose that during the course of an interview the interviewee demands in a very rude way that she be permitted to talk to your supervisor or someone in charge.
    Which of the following is probably the BEST way to handle this situation?
    A. Inform your supervisor of the demand and ask her to speak to the interviewee
    B. Pay no attention to the demands of the interviewee and continue the interview
    C. Report to your supervisor and tell her to get another interviewer for this interviewee
    D. Tell her you are the one "in charge" and that she should talk to you

16. Suppose that a worker asks a client to answer several required but rather personal questions about the family's health history. The client delays and seems embarrassed about giving the answers.
    Of the following, the MOST reasonable response to the client is one which
    A. shows an awareness of the client's efforts to hide something
    B. demonstrates the worker's qualifications for asking such questions
    C. allows this client to be excused from answering the questions
    D. convinces the client that his uneasiness in the situation is understood

16._____

17. A representative from a planned parenthood group comes to see you to get information for a community education program.
    You should
    A. check out this group to make sure it is not promoting zero population growth for minority groups
    B. develop a good relationship with him so as to provide better service to clients
    C. make sure they will not encourage unnecessary abortions
    D. refuse to see him

17._____

18. A member of a clerical training program is continually late to classes. He explains to you that he has a hard time getting up and asks that you report him on time because he needs to train for a job.
    What should your response be?
    A. Tell him that you get there on time and so should he
    B. Tell him that you do not lie for anyone
    C. Explain that it is your duty to keep accurate records and refer him to a counselor
    D. Tell him that you will cooperate with him but he has to try to do better

18._____

19. In a community meeting to explain a new agency policy, you find that the audience has no questions about the policy or your explanations.
    What would be the MOST appropriate response to the silence?
    A. Leave right away before they think of questions
    B. Thank the audience for their attention and assure them that you will be available if there are any questions later
    C. Ask several members in the audience if they understand the new policy
    D. Explain that the audience could not possibly understand all of the policy and they must have questions

19._____

20. Assume that you are confronted by an angry member of the public who has not been able to obtain the information he needs from your office. You do not know the answer to his question.
    The BEST thing for you to do would be to
    A. tell him to come back another time, after you have looked up the information
    B. check with your supervisor to find the correct answer

20._____

C. tell him to ask in another office, so that you will not lose time looking for the information
D. make up and answer to keep the man satisfied until the right answer is found

---

KEY (CORRECT ANSWERS)

1.	C	11.	C
2.	D	12.	C
3.	C	13.	C
4.	C	14.	A
5.	C	15.	A
6.	C	16.	D
7.	C	17.	B
8.	A	18.	C
9.	A	19.	B
10.	B	20.	B

EXAMINATION SECTION
TEST 1

DIRECTIONS: Each question or incomplete statement is followed by several suggested answers or completions. Select the one that BEST answers the question or completes the statement. *PRINT THE LETTER OF THE CORRECT ANSWER IN THE SPACE AT THE RIGHT.*

1. Of the following, an important goal of the reorganization of a human services agency is to

    A. strengthen the centralization of services at agency headquarters
    B. provide services within the neighborhoods according to local needs
    C. equalize the distribution of responsibilities between headquarters and neighborhood offices
    D. give more authority and responsibility to neighborhood offices than to headquarters

2. The one of the following which is NOT a purpose of the movement toward decentralization of city government is to

    A. reduce citizen alienation
    B. bolster city services
    C. respond to local needs
    D. discourage the local power structure

3. Of the following, the MOST desirable way to strengthen the capacity of communities to contribute to the solution of their own problems is to

    A. encourage participation of local residents in service planning and delivery
    B. establish city-wide job training programs
    C. reduce technical assistance to local small business so that they will learn by experience
    D. make local residents accountable to government agencies for funds and services provided

4. In organizing the residents of a disadvantaged neighborhood to develop projects for community improvement, the MOST effective of the following approaches is to

    A. concentrate on the group with most members
    B. devote more attention to groups which have vested interests
    C. try to include all groups
    D. give special consideration to official groups

5. The one of the following which has been the MOST common problem which occurs when attempts are made to obtain community participation in a project such as a neighborhood improvement program is

    A. domination by an aggressive but unrepresentative group
    B. public opposition by representatives of government agencies
    C. fragmentation and disruption of community services
    D. serious deterioration in the quality of services

6. Of the following, the MOST important aim of the community organizer in his early contacts with a community group should be to

   A. build a core of common interests
   B. establish himself as a forceful leader who can make decisions
   C. inform the group of its legal rights
   D. curb discussion of opposing viewpoints in order to develop harmonious relations

7. The one of the following which is the BEST method of encouraging neighborhood people to attend a community meeting is to

   A. send out notices at least a week in advance
   B. set up an agenda that deals with issues of serious local concern
   C. invite a prominent public figure to address the meeting
   D. send invitations to community people with similar viewpoints on the problem to be discussed

8. A basic difference between pure experimental research and action research is that experimental research is primarily concerned with the analysis of data for scientific or technological generalization, while action research is

   A. based on the results of trial and error
   B. designed to effect improvement in an on–going process
   C. intuitive rather than scientific in nature
   D. primarily concerned with the analysis of data for universal generalization

9. Assume that a community worker is assigned to organize a client group to participate in planning for services they particularly need.
   Of the following, it would be LEAST important for the organizer to become familiar with the

   A. local store owners   B. neighborhood resources
   C. potential leaders   D. informal leaders

10. Of the following, the factor which is MOST important in encouraging a high level of local participation in community projects is the

    A. degree of sophistication of the local people
    B. attitudes of the community development workers towards the local people
    C. amount of money available for training
    D. amount of time available for stimulation of community interest

11. Assume that you are the discussion leader of a meeting of a group of residents of a poverty area, many of whom are against a proposal to locate a methadone maintenance treatment center in the neighborhood.
    The BEST way for you to assist the group is to help them FIRST to

    A. get to know each other on an informal basis
    B. understand the overall background of the drug problem and the need for such a facility in the community
    C. concentrate on all the issues until they iron out conflicting viewpoints
    D. discuss the pros and cons briefly, take a vote, and accept the decision of the majority

12. Of the following, the MOST important aim of the community development process is primarily to strengthen the

    A. long-established social and political pattern of relationships
    B. influence of dominant ethnic and religious groups
    C. long-standing power of traditional central government
    D. positive impulses of people working toward a common goal

13. One method of influencing human behavior is based upon an optimistic belief in human potential for development and betterment.
    Workers in the human services who apply this method expect that it will

    A. awaken initiative in clients
    B. demand a pre-chosen response from clients
    C. give clients a spirit of competition
    D. get clients to accept new ideas

14. The community development process is MOST effective when

    A. final decisions are made solely by the community development expediters
    B. a firm plan is made after a project gets under way
    C. decisions are left in the hands of community people
    D. militant factions are permitted to take a firm stand

15. Of the following, the MOST significant indication that an organizer of a community group has done an effective job would be a situation where the group

    A. continues to grow in size and strength after the organizer has departed
    B. disperses after the organizer has departed because it has fulfilled its purpose
    C. attains its goals only under the organizer's guidance
    D. has a warm and friendly relationship with the organizer

16. The MAIN purpose of group discussion of community issues by local residents is to

    A. present a predetermined point of view
    B. provide an outlet for release of the participants' aggressions
    C. consider and work through common problems
    D. improve relationships among participants

17. Of the following, the MOST important reason why the community development worker in a disadvantaged community of a major metropolis should seek to understand the motivations of the local residents is that he will be more capable of assisting them in developing

    A. self-help activities
    B. projects which will get publicity
    C. an overall master plan
    D. projects which do not require technical assistance

18. At certain times, there is a tendency for community groups to disregard democratic procedures in making decisions, particularly in a situation where

    A. action depends on availability of community services
    B. the executive board makes the decision
    C. there is need for speedy action
    D. there is no sound basis for the decision

18.____

19. The employment of residents of poverty areas with little or no educational qualifications to assist professional staff members in working with clients of human services agencies is GENERALLY considered

    A. *advisable,* mainly because local paraprofessionals can be expected to bridge the gap between the middle class professional worker and lower class recipients of service
    B. *inadvisable,* mainly because the employment of workers who are not professionals will lower the professional standards of the agency's staff
    C. *advisable,* mainly because employment of paraprofes–sional local residents will save agency funds
    D. *inadvisable,* mainly because clients will receive services of poorer quality than services provided by professional workers

19.____

20. The social work activist who was a leader in the movement to achieve welfare reform by organizing welfare clients and encouraging the poor to demand their legal rights to public assistance is (was)

    A. Saul Alinsky   B. Richard Cloward
    C. Bertram Beck   D. Jesse Gray

20.____

Questions 21–26.

DIRECTIONS: Questions 21 through 26 are to be answered SOLELY on the basis of the following passage.

Too often in the past, society has accepted the existing social welfare programs, preferring to tinker with refinements when fundamental reform was in order. It has been a *demeaning*, degrading welfare system in which the instrument of government was wrongfully and *ineptly* used. It has been a system which has only alienated those forced to benefit from it and demoralized those who had to administer it at the level where the pain was clearly visible.

There is a need to put this nation on a course in which cash benefits, providing a basic level or support, are conferred in such a way as to intrude as little as possible into privacy and self–respect. It is difficult to define a basic level of support, no matter how high or low it might be set. In the end, however, the decision is not determined so much by how much is truly adequate for a family to meet all of its needs, but by the resources available to carry out the promise. That may be a harsh fact of life but it is also just that—a fact of life.

21. Of the following, the MOST suitable title for the above passage would be   21.____

    A. THE NEED FOR GOVERNMENT CONTROL OF WELFARE
    B. DETERMINING THE BASIC LEVEL OF SUPPORT
    C. THE NEED FOR WELFARE REFORM
    D. THE ELIMINATION OF WELFARE PROGRAMS

22. In this passage, the author's GREATEST criticism of the welfare system is that it is too   22.____

    A. disrespectful of recipients
    B. expensive to administer
    C. limited by regulations
    D. widespread in application

23. According to the passage, the basic level of support is ACTUALLY determined by   23.____

    A. how much is required for a family to meet all of its needs
    B. the age of the recipients
    C. how difficult it is to administer the program
    D. the economic resources of the nation

24. In this passage, the author does NOT argue for   24.____

    A. a work Incentive system   B. a basic level of support
    C. cash benefits   D. the privacy of recipients

25. As used in the above passage, the italicized word *demeaning* means MOST NEARLY   25.____

    A. ineffective   B. expensive
    C. overburdened   D. humiliating

26. As used in the above passage, the italicized word *ineptly* means MOST NEARLY   26.____

    A. foolishly   B. unsuccessfully
    C. unskillfully   D. unhappily

Questions 27-30.

DIRECTIONS: Questions 27 through 30 are to be answered SOLELY on the basis of the following paragraph.

The unemployment rate, which counts those unemployed in the sense that they are actively looking for work and unable to find it, gives a relatively *superficial* index of economic conditions in a community. A better index is the subemployment rate which includes the unemployment rate and also includes those working part-time while they are trying to get full-time work; those heads of households under 65 years of age who earn less than $240 per week working full-time, and those individuals under 65 who are not heads of households and earn less than $220 per week in a full-time job; and an estimate of the males *not counted*, which is a very real concern in ghetto areas.

27. Of the following, the MOST suitable title for the above paragraph would be

    A. EMPLOYMENT IN THE UNITED STATES
    B. PART-TIME WORKERS AND THE ECONOMY
    C. THE LABOR MARKET AND THE COMMUNITY
    D. TWO INDICATORS OF ECONOMIC CONDITIONS

28. On the basis of the paragraph, which of the following statements is CORRECT? The

    A. unemployment rate includes everyone who is not fully employed
    B. subemployment rate is higher than the unemployment rate
    C. unemployment rate gives a more complex picture of the economic situation than the subemployment rate
    D. subemployment rate indicates how many part-time workers are dissatisfied with the number of hours they work per week

29. As used in the above paragraph, the italicized word *superficial* means MOST NEARLY

    A. exaggerated   B. official
    C. surface   D. current

30. According to the paragraph, which of the following is included in the subemployment rate?

    A. Everyone who is unemployed
    B. All part-time workers
    C. Everyone under 65 who earns less than $224 per week in a full-time job
    D. All heads of households who earn less than $240 per week in a full-time job

KEY (CORRECT ANSWERS)

1. B	11. B	21. C
2. D	12. D	22. A
3. A	13. A	23. D
4. C	14. C	24. A
5. A	15. A	25. D
6. A	16. C	26. C
7. B	17. A	27. D
8. B	18. C	28. B
9. A	19. A	29. C
10. B	20. B	30. C

TEST 2

DIRECTIONS: Each question or incomplete statement is followed by several suggested answers or completions. Select the one that BEST answers the question or completes the statement. *PRINT THE LETTER OF THE CORRECT ANSWER IN THE SPACE AT THE RIGHT.*

1. The one of the following which accounts for the LARGEST portion of the budget of the Human Resources Administration is

    A. personnel and support services
    B. public assistance and medicaid
    C. services to children and youth
    D. community organization and development

    1.____

2. According to the latest statistics published by the U. S. Department of Health, Education and Welfare, the state which spent the LARGEST amount of money per person for public assistance is

    A. California
    B. Massachusetts
    C. Pennsylvania
    D. New York

    2.____

3. According to the MOST recent U.S. Census Bureau Report, the group living in New York City which has the lowest income level is the

    A. Blacks
    B. Puerto Ricans
    C. Dominicans
    D. Haitians

    3.____

4. The group that contains the LARGEST number of individuals receiving public assistance is

    A. children under working age
    B. unemployed heads of families
    C. the aged, disabled, and blind
    D. unemployed single persons

    4.____

5. A MAJOR difficulty faced by new arrivals to cities since 1970 which did not exist for earlier European immigrants is the fact that the majority of present–day arrivals

    A. must forfeit their native culture patterns
    B. have an obviously darker skin color than most longtime residents
    C. have little education
    D. have few occupational skills

    5.____

6. Generally speaking, low–income persons do not make maximum use of opportunities and services available to them MAINLY because

    A. most paraprofessional workers, while sincere in the desire to serve, are unable to reach the hard core
    B. much of the routine paperwork in public assistance programs is now assigned to paraprofessional workers
    C. they have become increasingly self–reliant and prefer to cope with their problems without help
    D. they lack the confidence and know–how necessary to make their needs known to the proper persons or agencies

    6.____

7. The one of the following problems which has once again become a serious concern of youth services agencies is the

   A. increasing high school drop-out rate
   B. resurgence of fighting youth gangs
   C. spread of youth narcotics addiction
   D. lack of recreation programs

8. Of the following, the MOST recent development with regard to welfare recipients is

   A. introduction of the declaration of need instead of an investigation of eligibility
   B. a major emphasis on employment programs
   C. increased use of casework therapy and psychiatric counseling
   D. acceptance of narcotics addicts for home relief

9. According to a recent decision by a federal court, regular reporting at state employment service offices to pick up checks or accept work can NO LONGER be required of recipients of

   A. Aid to the Disabled
   B. Home Relief
   C. Aid to Dependent Children
   D. Medicaid

10. A BASIC objective of the proposal for revenue sharing under consideration by the U.S. Congress is to provide

    A. state and local governments with new sources of revenue from the federal government and greater control over how this revenue is spent
    B. the federal government with greater control over spending of certain federally-raised tax revenues
    C. safeguards against improper allocation of funds by state and local officials and incentives to states for reporting violations by local government
    D. a method of sharing federal revenue with the states and localities in accordance with their required expenditures for public assistance and social welfare services

11. The component of the human services agency which sets policy for the administration, coordination, and allocation of funds for community action programs is the

    A. Community Development Agency
    B. Department of Social Services
    C. Council on Poverty
    D. Manpower and Career Development Agency

12. The policies of the Council Against Poverty are carried out by the

    A. Community Development Agency
    B. Manpower and Career Development Agency
    C. Department of Social Services
    D. Neighborhood Manpower Service Centers

13. The reorganization of the human services agency has established the unit of organization for provisions of services at the neighborhood level as the

   A. designated poverty area
   B. human resources district
   C. catchment area
   D. census tract

14. The Child Development Commission established by the Agency for Child Development can BEST be described as a group comprised of

   A. professionals in child psychology and early childhood education who will consult with Agency staff members on policy and programs
   B. parents, community organizations, and concerned citizens who will help the Agency determine, review, and modify policies and guidelines for childcare services
   C. child–care experts who will provide technical assistance to private groups that want to develop early childhood centers
   D. professionals who will offer health and nutrition consultation and a variety of support and referral services for children and parents

15. The BASIC purpose of the office of Community Social Services in the Department of Social Services is to

   A. help local community leaders establish liaison with private social service agencies in their communities
   B. determine the social service needs of each community and provide services in accordance with these needs
   C. provide information and referral to all HRA services existing in a particular community and to services provided by other city agencies and private organizations
   D. assume responsibility for a variety of social services mandated by federal and state regulations

16. The Social Service Exchange is CORRECTLY described as a

   A. recruitment center for the training and placement of volunteers for social and health agencies
   B. center which maintains a central index of case records of families and individuals known to social and health agencies
   C. center which provides information about and makes referrals to social and health agencies and proprietary nursing homes
   D. confidential advisory service to help potential contributors evaluate local voluntary health and welfare agencies

17. Which one of the following is an IMPORTANT purpose of the formation of the Office of Special Services for Children in the Department of Social Services?

   A. Greater programmatic integration of the protective and supportive services to children who are abused, neglected, dependent, delinquent, or in need of services
   B. More professional attention to child abuse cases and prompt court action to penalize parents of abused or neglected children
   C. Separation of programs and facilities for children adjudged to be delinquent from special services for other dependent, abused, or neglected children
   D. Increased attention to home–finding and foster care and adoption services rather than institutional care for dependent children

18. The one of the following which is provided by the Department of Social Services for current, former, and potential public assistance recipients ONLY is _____ services.

    A. information
    B. child welfare
    C. referral
    D. homemaker

19. A MAJOR goal of the Department of Social Services which is part of the reorganization and the separation of income maintenance from social services is to

    A. limit the provision of public social services to those persons who are eligible for public assistance
    B. make public social services available to all persons, whether or not they require financial assistance
    C. refer clients who require social services to private agencies wherever possible
    D. emphasize casework treatment and referral of clients for psychiatric services rather than programs to effect environmental change

20. Of the following, the MAIN functions of the Manpower and Career Development Agency (MCDA) of a human services agency are to

    A. train the unskilled, upgrade existing skills, develop job opportunities, and place newly–trained people in jobs
    B. operate manpower, recruitment, and testing centers under contract with private organizations
    C. provide remedial education and follow–up for dis–advantaged potential college students and vocational testing and counseling for veterans and ex–addicts
    D. provide job development, interviewing and placement, and manpower research services

Questions 21–25.

DIRECTIONS: Questions 21 through 25 are to be answered SOLELY on the diagram presented below.

HOW THE INNER-CITY FAMILY IN URBANVILLE SPENDS ITS MONEY

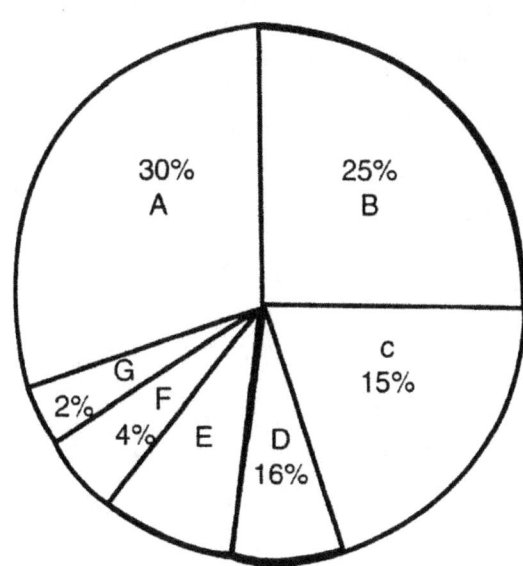

A. Food
B. Shelter
C. Clothing
D. Household Operation
E. Medical Care
F. Transportation
G. Miscellaneous

21. According to the above diagram, the percentage spent on medical care is   21.____

    A. 7%   B. 8%   C. 16%   D. 18%

22. According to the above diagram, the total percentage spent on food, shelter, and clothing is   22.____

    A. 55%   B. 60%   C. 70%   D. 75%

23. In a typical period, if the family spent $60 on transportation, how much did it spend on household operation?   23.____

    A. $240   B. $384   C. $600   D. $960

24. If the family income is $250 a week, how much does it spend on transportation each year?   24.____

    A. $120   B. $520   C. $1,200   D. $5,200

25. Assume that the annual income of a family was $10,800 for several years. Last year, the income went up 5%, and the family then tripled the typical percentage for household operation.   25.____
    The amount spent on this item last year was MOST NEARLY

    A. $1,782   B. $2,268   C. $2,592   D. $5,442

Questions 26–30.

DIRECTIONS: Questions 26 through 30 are to be answered SOLELY on the basis of the table presented below.

AFDC FAMILY MEMBERS IN URBANVILLE
Referred to and Enrolled in WIN Program, 2001-2002

	Referred		Enrolled	
Family Member	2001	2002	2001	2002
Mother	1,091	1,306	730	877
Father	743	950	520	731
Child, age 16 and over	170	222	150	184

26. According to the above table, how many AFDC family members were referred to WIN in 2002?

    A. 1,792   B. 2,004   C. 2,388   D. 2,478

27. According to the above table, the number of AFDC children 16 and over who were enrolled in WIN in 2002 was GREATER than the number enrolled in 2001 by

    A. 12   B. 34   C. 38   D. 52

28. According to the above table, the number of AFDC mothers who were enrolled in 2002 INCREASED over the number enrolled in 2001 MOST NEARLY by

    A. 20%   B. 32%   C. 54%   D. 83%

29. In 2003, if the number of AFDC mothers referred to WIN increases 5% over 2002, the number of fathers referred increases 8% over 2002, and the number of children referred increases 5% over 2002, the TOTAL number of AFDC family members that will be referred in 2003 is MOST NEARLY

    A. 1,424   B. 1,524   C. 3,130   D. 3,990

30. According to the above table, the percentage of AFDC fathers NOT enrolled in WIN in 2002 of the number referred that year is MOST NEARLY

    A. 23%   B. 25%   C. 71%   D. 77%

KEY (CORRECT ANSWERS)

1.	B	11.	C	21.	B
2.	D	12.	A	22.	C
3.	D	13.	B	23.	A
4.	A	14.	B	24.	B
5.	B	15.	B	25.	D
6.	D	16.	B	26.	D
7.	B	17.	A	27.	B
8.	B	18.	D	28.	A
9.	C	19.	B	29.	C
10.	A	20.	A	30.	A

EXAMINATION SECTION
TEST 1

DIRECTIONS: Each question or incomplete statement is followed by several suggested answers or completions. Select the l one that BEST answers the question or completes the statement. *PRINT THE LETTER OF THE CORRECT ANSWER IN THE SPACE AT THE RIGHT.*

1. The applicant you are interviewing is a man in his late forties who has recently lost his job and has a family of eight to support. He is very upset and tells you he does not know where he will get the money to purchase food for the family and pay the rent. He does not know what he will do if he is found not eligible for public assistance. He asks you whether you think he will be eligible. You feel the applicant has a good chance, and you think he should receive financial assistance, but you are not completely certain that he is eligible for public assistance under departmental policy.
Of the following, the BEST action for you to take is to

   A. reassure the applicant and tell him you are sure everything will be all right because there is no sense in worrying him before you know for certain that he is not eligible
   B. tell the applicant that as far as you are concerned he should receive public assistance but that you are not certain the department will go along with your recommendation
   C. tell the applicant that you are not sure that he will be found eligible for public assistance
   D. adopt a cool manner and tell the applicant that he must behave like an adult and not allow himself to become emotional about the situation

1.____

2. When conducting an interview with a client receiving public assistance, it would be LEAST important for you to try to

   A. understand the reasons for the client's statements
   B. conduct the interview on the client's intellectual level
   C. imitate the client's speech as much as possible
   D. impress the client with the agency's concern for his welfare

2.____

Questions 3-6.

DIRECTIONS: Questions 3 through 6 are to be answered SOLELY on basis of the following case history of the Foster family.

FOSTER CASE HISTORY

Form W-341-C
Rev. 3/1/03
600M-804077-S-200 (93)-245

Date: Jan. 25, 2015
Case Name: Foster
Case No. : ADC-3415968

Family Composition: Ann Foster, b. 7.23.77
Gerry b. 1.7.02
Susan b. 4.1.04
John b. 5.3.07
Joan b. 10.14.10

Mrs. Foster was widowed in June 2011 when her husband was killed in a car accident. Since that time, the family has received public assistance. Mrs. Foster has been referred for housekeeping service by the Social Service Department of Lincoln Hospital, where she is being treated in the neurology clinic. Her primary diagnosis is multiple sclerosis. The hospital reports that she is going through a period of deterioration characterized by an unsteady gait, and weakness and tremor in the limbs. At this time, her capacity to manage a household and four children is severely limited. She feels quite overwhelmed and is unable to function adequately in taking care of her home.

In addition to the medical reasons, it is advisable that a housekeeper be placed in the home as part of a total plan to avoid further family breakdown and deterioration. This deterioration is reflected by all family members. Mrs. Foster is severely depressed and is unable to meet the needs of her children, who have a variety of problems. Joan, the youngest, is not speaking, is hyperactive, and in general is not developing normally for a child her age. John is showing learning problems in school and has poor articulation. Susan was not promoted last year and is a behavior problem at home. Gerry, the oldest, is deformed due to a fire at age two. It is clear that Mrs. Foster cannot control or properly discipline her children, but even more important is the fact that she is unable to offer them the encouragement and guidance they require.

It is hoped that providing housekeeping service will relieve Mrs. Foster of the basic household chores so that she will be less frustrated and better able to provide the love and guidance needed by her children.

3. The age of the child who is described as not developing normally, hyperactive, and not speaking is

   A. 4   B. 7   C. 10   D. 13

4. Which of the following CANNOT be verified on the basis of the Foster Case History above?

   A. William Foster was Ann Foster's husband.
   B. Mrs. Foster has been seen in the neurology clinic at Lincoln Hospital.
   C. John Foster has trouble with his speech.
   D. The Foster family has received public assistance since June 2011.

5. The form on which the information about the Foster family is presented is known as

   A. Family Composition Form   B. Form Rev. 3/1/03
   C. Form W-341-C   D. ADC-3415968

6. According to the above case history, housekeeping service is being requested PRIMARILY because 6.____

    A. no one in the family can perform the household chores
    B. Mrs. Foster suffers from multiple sclerosis and requires assistance with the household chores
    C. the children are exhibiting behavior problems resulti from the mother's illness
    D. the children have no father

7. You notice that an applicant whom you rejected for public assistance is back at the center the following morning and is waiting to be interviewed by another worker in your group. 7.____
Of the following, the BEST approach for you to take is to

    A. inform the worker, before she interviews the applicant that you had interviewed and rejected him the previous day
    B. not inform the worker about the situation and let her make her own decision
    C. approach the applicant and tell him he was rejected for good reason and will have to leave the center immediately
    D. ask the special officer at the center to remove the applicant

8. You have just finished interviewing an applicant who has a violent temper and has displayed a great amount of hostility toward you during the interview. You find he is ineligible for public assistance. Departmental policy is that all applicants are notified by mail in a day or so of their acceptance or rejection for public assistance. However, you also have the option, if you think it is desirable, of notifying the applicant at the interview. 8.____
Of the following, the BEST action for you to take in this case is to

    A. tell the applicant of his rejection during the interview
    B. have the applicant notified of the results of the interview by mail only
    C. ask your supervisor to inform the applicant of his rejection
    D. inform the applicant of the results of the interview, with a special patrolman at your side

9. You are interviewing a client who speaks English poorly and whose native language is Spanish. Your knowledge of Spanish is very limited. 9.____
Of the following, the FIRST action it would be best for you to take is to

    A. try to locate a worker at the center who speaks Spanish
    B. write our your questions because it is easier for people to understand a new language when it is written rather than when it is spoken
    C. do the best you can, using hand gestures to make yourself understood
    D. tell the client to return with a friend or relative who speaks English

10. During an interview with a client of another race, he accuses you of racial prejudice and asks for an interviewer of his own race. 10.____
Of the following, which is the BEST way to handle the situation?

    A. In a friendly manner, tell the client that eligibility is based on the regulations and the facts, not on prejudice, and ask him to continue with the interview.
    B. Explain to your supervisor that you cannot deal with someone who accuses you of prejudice, and ask your supervisor to assign the client someone of his own race.
    C. Assure the client that you will lean over backwards to treat his application favorably.

D. Tell the client that some of your friends are of his race and that you could therefore not possibly be prejudiced.

Questions 11-15.

DIRECTIONS: In order to answer Questions 11 through 15, assume that you have been asked to write a short report on the basis of the information contained in the following passage about the granting of emergency funds to the Smith family.

Mr. and Mrs. Smith, who have been receiving public assistance for the last six months, arrive at the center the morning of August 2, totally upset and anxious because they and their family have been burned out of their apartment the night before. The fire seems to have been of suspicious origin because at the time it broke out witnesses spotted two neighborhood teenagers running away from the scene. The policemen, who arrived at the scene shortly after the firemen, took down the pertinent information about the alleged arsonists.

The Smiths have spent the night with friends but now request emergency housing and emergency funds for themselves and their four children to purchase food and to replace the clothing which was destroyed by the fire. The burned-out apartment had consisted of 5 rooms and a bath, and the Smiths are now worried that they will be forced to accept smaller accommodations. Furthermore, since Mrs. Smith suffers from a heart murmur, she is worried that their new living quarters will necessitate her climbing too many stairs. Her previous apartment was a one-flight walk-up, which was acceptable.

As the worker in charge, you have studied the case, determined the amount of the emergency grant, made temporary arrangements for the Smiths to stay at a hotel, and reassured Mrs. Smith that everything possible will be done to find them an apartment which will meet with their approval.

11. Which of the following would it be BEST to include in the report as the reason for the emergency grant?

    A. The police have decided that the fire is of suspicious origin.
    B. Two neighborhood teenagers were seen leaving the fire at the Smiths'.
    C. The apartment of the Smith family has been destroyed by fire.
    D. Mrs. Smith suffers from a heart murmur and cannot climb stairs.

12. Which of the following would it be BEST to accept as verification of the fire?
    A

    A. letter from the friends with whom the Smiths stayed the previous night
    B. photograph of the fire
    C. dated newspaper clipping describing the fire
    D. note from the Smiths' neighbors

13. A report of the Smith family's need for a new apartment must be sent to the center's housing specialist.
    Which of the following recommendations for housing would be MOST appropriate?

    A. Two bedrooms, first floor walk-up
    B. Five rooms, ground floor
    C. Two-room suite, hotel with elevator
    D. Three rooms, building with elevator

14. For which of the following are the Smiths requesting emergency funds?　　　　14.____

    A. Furniture 　　　　　　　　　　B. Food
    C. A hotel room　　　　　　　　　 D. Repairs in their apartment

15. Which of the following statements provides the BEST summary of the action taken by　15.____
    you on the Smith case and is MOST important for inclusion in your report?

    A. Mr. and Mrs. Smith arrived upset and anxious and were reassured.
    B. It was verified that there was a fire.
    C. Temporary living arrangements were made, and the amount of the emergency grant was determined.
    D. The case was studied and a new apartment was found for the Smiths which met with their approval.

16. It is important that you remember what has happened between you and a client during　16.____
    an interview so that you may deliver appropriate services.
    However, the one of the following which is the MOST likely reason that taking notes during the interview may not always be a good practice is that

    A. you may lose the notes and have to go back and see the client again
    B. some clients may believe that you are not interested in what they are saying
    C. you are the only one who is likely to read the notes
    D. some clients may believe that you are not smart enough to remember what happened in the interview

17. Before an applicant seeking public assistance can be interviewed, he must fill out a complex　17.____
    application form which consists of eleven pages of questions requesting very detailed information.
    Of the following, the BEST time for you to review the information on the application form is

    A. before she begins to interview the applicant
    B. after she has asked the applicant a few questions to put him at ease
    C. towards the end of the interview so that she has a chance to think about the information received during the interview
    D. after the interview has been completed

Questions 18-20.

DIRECTIONS:　In Questions 18 through 20, choose the lettered word which means MOST NEARLY the same as the underlined word in the sentence.

18. He needed public assistance because he was incapacitated. The word incapacitated　18.____
    means MOST NEARLY

    A. uneducated　　　　　　　　　B. disabled
    C. uncooperative　　　　　　　　D. discharged

19. The caseworker explained to the client that signing the document was compulsory.　19.____
    The word compulsory means MOST NEARLY

    A. temporary　　　　　　　　　　B. required
    C. different　　　　　　　　　　　D. comprehensive

20. The woman's actions did not jeopardize her eligibility for benefits. 20.____
    The word jeopardize means MOST NEARLY

    A. delay   B. reinforce   C. determine   D. endanger

KEY (CORRECT ANSWERS)

1.	C	11.	C
2.	C	12.	C
3.	A	13.	B
4.	A	14.	B
5.	C	15.	C
6.	B	16.	B
7.	A	17.	A
8.	B	18.	B
9.	A	19.	B
10.	A	20.	D

TEST 2

DIRECTIONS: Each question or incomplete statement is followed by several suggested answers or completions. Select the one that BEST answers the question or completes the statement. *PRINT THE LETTER OF THE CORRECT ANSWER IN THE SPACE AT THE RIGHT.*

Questions 1-4.

DIRECTIONS: Questions 1 through 4 are to be answered on the basis of the information given in the Fact Situation and Sample Form below.

FACT SITUATION

On October 7, 2014, John Smith (Case #ADC-U 1467912) applied and was accepted for public assistance for himself and his family. His family consists of his wife, Helen, and their children: William, age 9; John Jr., age 6; and Mary, age 2. The family has lived in a five-room apartment located at 142 West 137 Street, Manhattan, since July 18, 2008. Mr. Smith signed a 2-year lease for this apartment on July 18, 2014 at a rent of $500 per month. The maximum rental allowance for a family of this size is $420 per month. Utilities are included in this rent-controlled multiple dwelling.

Since the cost of renting this apartment is in excess of the allowable amount, the Supervising Clerk (Income Maintenance) is required to fill out a "Request for Approval of Exception to Policy for Shelter Allowance/Rehousing Expenses."

A sample of a section of this form follows.

SAMPLE FORM

REQUEST FOR APPROVAL OF EXCEPTION TO POLICY FOR SHELTER ALLOWANCE /REHOUSING EXPENSES

Case Name	Case No. or Pending		Acceptance Date	Group No.	
Present Address ZIP	Apt. No. or Location	No. of Rooms	Rent per Mo. $	Occupancy Date	
HOUSEHOLD COMPOSITION (List all persons living in the household) Column I Surname First	Col. 2 Birth-date	Col. 3 Sex	Column 4 Relation to Case Head	Column 5 Marital Status	Column 6 P. A. Status

1. Based on the information given in the Fact Situation, which one of the following should be entered in the space for *Occupancy Date*?

    A. October 7, 2014
    B. July 18, 2014
    C. July 18, 2008
    D. Unknown

2. What amount should be entered in the space labeled *Rent per Mo.* ?

    A. $500
    B. $420
    C. $300
    D. $80

3. Based on the information given in the Fact Situation, it is IMPOSSIBLE to fill in which one of the following blanks?

    A. *Case Number or pending*
    B. *Acceptance Date*
    C. *Apt. No. or Location*
    D. *No. of Rooms*

4. Which of the following should be entered in Column 4 for Helen Smith?

    A. Wife
    B. Head
    C. Mother
    D. Unknown

Questions 5-13.

DIRECTIONS: In Questions 5 through 13, perform the computations indicated and choose the CORRECT answer from the four choices given.

5. Add $4.34, $34.50, $6.00, $101.76, $90.67. From the result, subtract $60.54 and $10.56.

    A. $76.17
    B. $156.37
    C. $166.17
    D. $300.37

6. Add 2,200, 2,600, 252, and 47.96.
   From the result, subtract 202.70, 1,200, 2,150, and 434.43.

    A. 1,112.83
    B. 1,213.46
    C. 1,341.51
    D. 1,348.91

7. Multiply 1850 by .05 and multiply 3300 by .08 and then add both results.

    A. 242.50
    B. 264.00
    C. 333.25
    D. 356.50

8. Multiply 312.77 by .04.
   Round off the result to the nearest hundredth.

    A. 12.52
    B. 12.511
    C. 12.518
    D. 12.51

9. Add 362.05, 91.13, 347.81, and 17.46, and then divide the result by 6.
   The answer rounded off to the nearest hundredth is

    A. 138.409
    B. 137.409
    C. 136.41
    D. 136.40

10. Add 66.25 and 15.06, and then multiply the result by 2 1/6.
    The answer is MOST NEARLY

    A. 176.18
    B. 176.17
    C. 162.66
    D. 162.62

11. Each of the following options contains three decimals. In which case do all three decimals have the same value?

    A. .3; .30; .03
    B. .25; .250; .2500
    C. 1.9; 1.90; 1.09
    D. .35; .350; .035

12. Add 1/2 the sum of (539.84 and 479.26) to 1/3 the sum of (1461.93 and 927.27). 12._____
    Round off the result to the nearest whole number.

    A. 3408 B. 2899 C. 1816 D. 1306

13. Multiply $5,906.09 by 15%, and then divide the result by 1/3. 13._____

    A. $295.30 B. $885.91 C. $8,859.14 D. $29,530.45

Questions 14-18.

DIRECTIONS: Questions 14 through 18 are to be answered SOLELY on the basis of the information provided in the following passage.

The ideal relationship for the interview is one of mutual confidence. To try to pretend, to put on a front of cordiality and friendship is extremely unwise for the interviewer because he will certainly convey, by subtle means, his real feelings. It is the interviewer's responsibility to take the lead in establishing a relationship of mutual confidence.

As the interviewer, you should help the interviewee to feel at ease and ready to talk. One of the best ways to do this is to be at ease yourself. If you are, it will probably be evident; if you are not, it will almost certainly be apparent to the interviewee.

Begin the interview with topics for discussion which are easy to talk about and non-menacing. This interchange can be like the conversation of people when they are waiting for a bus, at the ball game, or discussing the weather. However, do not prolong this warm-up too long since the interviewee knows as well as you do that these are not the things he came to discuss. Delaying too long in getting down to business may suggest to him that you are reluctant to deal with the topic.

Once you get onto the main topics, do all that you can to get the interviewee to talk freely with as little prodding from you as possible. This will probably require that you give him some idea of the area, and of ways of looking at it. Avoid, however, prejudicing or coloring his remarks by what you say; especially, do not in any way indicate that there are certain things you want to hear, others which you do not want to hear. It is essential that he feel free to express his own ideas unhampered by your ideas, your values and preconceptions.

Do not appear to dominate the interview, nor have even the suggestion of a patronizing attitude. Ask some questions which will enable the interviewee to take pride in his knowledge. Take the attitude that the interviewee sincerely wants the interview to achieve its purpose. This creates a warm, permissive atmosphere that is most important in all interviews.

14. Of the following, the BEST title for the above passage is 14._____

    A. PERMISSIVENESS IN INTERVIEWING
    B. INTERVIEWING TECHNIQUES
    C. THE FACTOR OF PRETENSE IN THE INTERVIEW
    D. THE CORDIAL INTERVIEW

15. Which of the following recommendations on the conduct of an interview is made by the above passage?

    A. Conduct the interview as if it were an interchange between people discussing the weather.
    B. The interview should be conducted in a highly impersonal manner.
    C. Allow enough time for the interview so that the interviewee does not feel rushed.
    D. Start the interview with topics which are not threatening to the interviewee.

16. The above passage indicates that the interviewer should

    A. feel free to express his opinions
    B. patronize the interviewee and display a permissive attitude
    C. permit the interviewee to give the needed information in his own fashion
    D. provide for privacy when conducting the interview

17. The meaning of the word *unhampered,* as it is used in the last sentence of the fourth paragraph of the preceding passage, is MOST NEARLY

    A. unheeded   B. unobstructed
    C. hindered   D. aided

18. It can be INFERRED from the above passage that

    A. interviewers, while generally mature, lack confidence
    B. certain methods in interviewing are more successful than others in obtaining information
    C. there is usually a reluctance on the part of interviewers to deal with unpleasant topics
    D. it is best for the interviewer not to waiver from the use of hard and fast rules when dealing with clients

19. The applicant whom you are interviewing is not talking rationally, and he admits that he is under the influence of alcohol.
    Which of the following is the BEST way of handling this situation?

    A. Call a security guard and have the applicant removed.
    B. Tell the applicant that unless he gets control of himself, he will not receive financial assistance.
    C. Send out for a cup of black coffee for the applicant.
    D. End the interview and plan to schedule another appointment.

20. During an interview, an applicant who has submitted an application for assistance breaks down and cries. Of the following, the BEST way of handling this situation is to

    A. end the interview and schedule a new appointment
    B. be patient and sympathetic, and encourage the applicant to continue the interview
    C. tell the applicant sternly that crying will not help matters
    D. tell the applicant that you will do everything you can to get the application approved

KEY (CORRECT ANSWERS)

1. C
2. A
3. C
4. A
5. C

6. A
7. D
8. D
9. C
10. B

11. B
12. D
13. A
14. B
15. D

16. C
17. B
18. B
19. D
20. B

INTERVIEWING
EXAMINATION SECTION
TEST 1

DIRECTIONS: Each question or incomplete statement is followed by several suggested answers or completions. Select the one that BEST answers the question or completes the statement. *PRINT THE LETTER OF THE CORRECT ANSWER IN THE SPACE AT THE RIGHT.*

1. Of the methods given below for obtaining desired information from applicants, the one considered the BEST interviewing method is to
   A. work from an outline, asking the questions in the order in which they appear and requiring the applicant to give specific answers
   B. let the applicant tell what he has to say in his own way first, the interviewer then taking responsibility for asking questions on points not covered
   C. tell the applicant all the facts that it is necessary to have, then letting him give the information in any way he chooses
   D. verify all such facts as birth date, income, and past employment before seeing the applicant, then asking the applicant to fill in the remaining gaps when he is interviewed

2. Suppose an applicant objects to answering a question regarding his recent employment and asks, "What business is it of yours, young man?"
   In conducting the interview, the MOST constructive course of action for you to take under the circumstances would be to
   A. tell the applicant you have no intention of prying into his personal affairs and go on to the next question
   B. refer the applicant to your supervisor
   C. rephrase the question so that only a "Yes" or "No" answer is required
   D. explain why the question is being asked

3. An interview is BEST conducted in private PRIMARILY because
   A. the person interviewed will tend to be less self-conscious
   B. the interviewer will be able to maintain his continuity of thought better
   C. it will insure that the interview is "off the record"
   D. people tend to "show off" before an audience

4. An interviewer will be better able to understand the person interviewed and his problems if he recognizes that much of the person's behavior is due to motives
   A. which are deliberate
   B. of which he is unaware
   C. which are inexplicable
   D. which are kept under control

5. When an applicant is repeatedly told that "everything will be all right," the effect that can USUALLY be expected is that he will
   A. develop overt negativistic reactions toward the agency
   B. become too closely identified with the interviewer
   C. doubt the interviewer's ability to understand and help with his problems
   D. have greater confidence in the interviewer

6. While interviewing a client, it is PREFERABLE that the interviewer
   A. take no notes in order to avoid disturbing the client
   B. focus primary attention on the client while the client is talking
   C. take no notes in order to impress upon the client the interviewer's ability to remember all the pertinent facts of his case
   D. record all the details in order to show the client that what he says is important

7. During an interview, a curious applicant asks several questions about the interviewer's private life.
   As the interviewer, you should
   A. refuse to answer such questions
   B. answer his questions fully
   C. explain that your primary concern is with his problems and that discussion of your personal affairs will not be helpful in meeting his needs
   D. explain that it is the responsibility of the interviewer to ask questions and not to answer them

8. An interviewer can BEST establish a good relationship with the person being interviewed by
   A. assuming casual interest in the statements made by the person being interviewed
   B. asking questions which enable the person to show pride in his knowledge
   C. taking the point of view of the person interviewed
   D. showing a genuine interest in the person

9. An interviewer's attention must be directed toward himself as well as toward the person interviewed.
   This statement means that the interviewer should
   A. keep in mind the extent to which his own prejudices may influence his judgment
   B. rationalize the statements made by the person interviewed
   C. gain the respect and confidence of the person interviewed
   D. avoid being too impersonal

10. More complete expression will be obtained from a person being interviewed if the interviewer can create the impression that
    A. the data secured will become part of a permanent record
    B. official information must be accurate in every detail
    C. it is the duty of the person interviewed to give accurate data
    D. the person interviewed is participating in a discussion of his own problems

11. The practice of asking leading questions should be avoided in an interview because the
    A. interviewer risks revealing his attitudes to the person being interviewed
    B. interviewer may be led to ignore the objective attitudes of the person interviewed
    C. answers may be unwarrantedly influenced
    D. person interviewed will resent the attempt to lead him and will be less cooperative

11.____

12. A good technique for the interviewer to use in an effort to secure reliable data and to reduce the possibility of misunderstanding is to
    A. use casual undirected conversation, enabling the person being interviewed to talk about himself, and thus secure the desired information
    B. adopt the procedure of using direct questions regularly
    C. extract the desired information from the person being interviewed by putting him on the defensive
    D. explain to the person being interviewed the information desired and the reason for needing it

12.____

13. In interviewing an applicant, your attitude toward his veracity should be that the information he has furnished you is
    A. *untruthful* until you have had an opportunity to check the information
    B. *truthful* only insofar as verifiable facts are concerned
    C. *untruthful* because clients tend to interpret everything in their own favor
    D. *truthful* until you have information to the contrary

13.____

14. When an agency assigns its most experienced interviewers to conduct initial interviews with applicants, the MOST important reason for its action is that
    A. experienced workers are always older and, therefore, command the respect of applicants
    B. the applicant may be given a complete understanding of the procedures to be followed and the time involved in obtaining assistance
    C. applicants with fraudulent intentions will be detected, and prevented from obtaining further services from the agency
    D. the applicant may be given an understanding of the purpose of the assistance program and of the bases for granting assistance, in addition to the routine information

14.____

15. In conducting the first interview with an applicant, you should
    A. ask questions requiring "Yes" or "No" answers in order to simplify the interview
    B. rephrase several of the key questions as a check on his previous statements
    C. let him tell his own story while keeping him to the relevant facts
    D. avoid showing any sympathy for the applicant while he is revealing his personal needs and problems

15.____

4 (#1)

16. When an interview opens an interview by asking the client direct questions about his work, it is very likely that the client will feel
    A. that the interview is interested in him
    B. at ease if his work has been good
    C. free to discuss his attitudes toward his work
    D. that good reports are of great importance to the interviewer in his thinking

16.____

17. When an interviewer does NOT understand the meaning of a response that a client has made, the interviewer should
    A. proceed to another topic
    B. state that he does not understand and ask for clarification
    C. act as if he understands so that the client's confidence in him should not be shaken
    D. ask the client to rephrase his response

17.____

18. When an interviewer makes a response which brings on a high degree of resistance in the client, he should
    A. apologize and rephrase his remark in a less evocative manner
    B. accept the resistance on the part of the client
    C. ignore the client's resistance
    D. recognize that little more will be accomplished in the interview and suggest another appointment

18.____

19. Most definitions of interviewing would NOT include the following as a necessary aspect:
    A. The interviewer and client meet face-to-face and talk things out
    B. The client is experiencing considerable emotional disturbance
    C. A valuable learning opportunity is provided for the client
    D. The interviewer brings a special competence to the relationship

19.____

20. A powerful dynamic in the interviewing process and often the very *antonym* of its counterpart in the instructional process is
    A. encouraging accuracy
    B. emphasizing structure
    C. pointing up sequential and orderly thinking
    D. processing ambiguity and equivocation

20.____

21. Interviewing techniques are frequently useful in working with clients. A basic fundamental is an atmosphere which may BEST be described as
    A. non-threatening
    B. motivating for creativity
    C. highly charged to stimulate excitement
    D. fairly-well structured

21.____

22. In interviewing the disadvantaged client, the subtle technique of steering away from high-level educational and vocational plans must be *replaced* by
    A. a wait-and-see explanation to the client
    B. the use of prediction tables to determine possibilities and probabilities of overcoming this condition

22.____

C. avoidance in discussing controversial issues of deprivation
D. encouragement and concrete consideration for planning his future

23. The process of collecting, analyzing, synthesizing, and interpreting information about the client should be
    A. completed prior to interviewing
    B. completed early in the interviewing process
    C. limited to a type of interviewing which is primarily diagnostic in purpose
    D. continuously pursued throughout interviewing

23.____

24. Catharsis, the "emotional unloading" of the client's feelings, has a value in the early stages of interviewing because it accomplishes all BUT which one of the following goals?
    It
    A. relieves strong physiological tensions in the client
    B. increases the client's anxiety and aggrandizes his motivation to continue counseling
    C. provides a strong substitute for "acting out" the client's feelings
    D. releases emotional energy which the client has been using to bulwark his defenses

24.____

25. In the interviewing process, the interviewer should *usually* give information
    A. whenever it is needed
    B. at the end of the process
    C. in the introductory interview
    D. just before the client would ordinarily request it

25.____

KEY (CORRECT ANSWERS)

1.	B	11.	C
2.	D	12.	D
3.	A	13.	D
4.	B	14.	D
5.	C	15.	C
6.	B	16.	D
7.	C	17.	B
8.	D	18.	B
9.	A	19.	B
10.	D	20.	D

21. A
22. D
23. D
24. B
25. A

TEST 2

DIRECTIONS: Each question or incomplete statement is followed by several suggested answers or completions. Select the one that BEST answers the question or completes the statement. *PRINT THE LETTER OF THE CORRECT ANSWER IN THE SPACE AT THE RIGHT.*

1. Of the following problems that might affect the conduct and outcome of an interview, the MOST troublesome and usually the MOST difficult for the interviewer to control is the
    A. tendency of the interviewee to anticipate the needs and preferences of the interviewer
    B. impulse to cut the interviewee off when he seems to have reached the end of an idea
    C. tendency of interviewee attitude to bias the results
    D. tendency of the interviewer to do most of the talking

    1.____

2. The supervisor MOST likely to be a good interviewer is one who
    A. is adept at manipulating people and circumstances toward his objective
    B. is able to put himself in the position of the interviewee
    C. gets the more difficult questions out of the way at the beginning of the interview
    D. develops one style and technique that can be used in any type of interview

    2.____

3. A good interviewer guards against the tendency to form an overall opinion about an interviewee on the basis of a single aspect of the interviewee's makeup.
    This statement refers to a well-known source of error in interviewing known as the
    A. assumption error   B. expectancy error
    C. extension effect   D. halo effect

    3.____

4. In conducting an "exit interview" with an employee who is leaving voluntarily, the interview's MAIN objective should be to
    A. see that the employee leaves with a good opinion of the organization
    B. learn the true reasons for the employee's resignation
    C. find out if the employee would consider a transfer
    D. try to get the employee to remain on the job

    4.____

5. During an interview, an interviewee unexpectedly discloses a relevant but embarrassing personal fact.
    It would be BEST for the interviewer to
    A. listen calmly, avoiding any gesture or facial expression that would suggest approval or disapproval of what is related
    B. change the subject, since further discussion in this area may reveal other embarrassing, but irrelevant, personal facts

    5.____

C. apologize to the interviewee for having led him to reveal such a fact and promise not to do so again
D. bring the interview to a close as quickly as possible in order to avoid a discussion which may be distressing to the interviewee

6. Suppose that, while you are interviewing an applicant for a position in your office, you notice a contradiction in facts in two of his responses.
For you to call the contradictions to his attention would be
    A. *inadvisable*, because it reduces the interviewee's level of participation
    B. *advisable*, because getting the facts is essential to a successful interview
    C. *inadvisable*, because the interviewer should use more subtle techniques to resolve any discrepancies
    D. *advisable*, because the interviewee should be impressed with the necessity for giving consistent answers

7. An interviewer should be aware that an undesirable result of including "leading questions" in an interview is to
    A. cause the interviewee to give a "yes" or "no" answers with qualification or explanation
    B. encourage the interviewee to discuss irrelevant topics
    C. encourage the interviewee to give more meaningful information
    D. reduce the validity of the information obtained from the interviewee

8. The kind of interview which is particularly helpful in getting an employee to tell about his complaints and grievances is one in which
    A. a pattern has been worked out involving a sequence of exact questions to be asked
    B. the interviewee is expected to support his statements with specific evidence
    C. the interviewee is not made to answer specific questions but is encouraged to talk freely
    D. the interviewer has specific items on which he wishes to get or give information

9. Suppose you are scheduled to interview an employee under your supervision concerning a health problem. You know that some of the questions you will be asking him will seem embarrassing to him, and that he may resist answering these questions.
In general, to hold these questions for the last part of the interview would be
    A. *desirable*; the intervening time period gives the interviewer an opportunity to plan how to ask these sensitive questions.
    B. *undesirable*; the employee will probably feel that he has been tricked when he suddenly must answer embarrassing questions
    C. *desirable*; the employee will probably have increased confidence in the interviewer and be more willing to answer these questions
    D. *undesirable*; questions that are important should not be deferred until the end of the interview

10. In conducting an interview, the BEST types of questions with which to begin the interview are those which the person interviewed is
    A. willing and able to answer
    B. willing but unable to answer
    C. able but unwilling to answer
    D. unable and unwilling to answer

10.____

11. In order to determine accurately a child's age, it is BEST for an interviewer to rely on
    A. the child's grade in school
    B. what the mother says
    C. birth records
    D. a library card

11.____

12. In his first interview with a new employee, it would be LEAST appropriate for a unit supervisor to
    A. find out the employee's preference for the several types of jobs to which he is able to assign him
    B. determine whether the employee will make good promotion material
    C. inform the employee of what his basic job responsibilities will be
    D. inquire about the employee's education and previous employment

12.____

13. If an interviewer takes care to phrase his questions carefully and precisely, the result will MOST probably be that
    A. he will be able to determine whether the person interviewed is being truthful
    B. the free flow of the interview will be lost
    C. he will get the information he wants
    D. he will ask stereotyped questions and narrow the scope of the interview

13.____

14. When, during an interview, is the person interviewed LEAST likely to be cautious about what he tells the interviewer?
    A. Shortly after the beginning when the questions normally suggest pleasant associations to the person interviewed
    B. As long as the interviewer keeps his questions to the point
    C. At the point where the person interviewed gains a clear insight into the area being discussed
    D. When the interview appears formally ended and goodbyes are being said

14.____

15. In an interview held for the purpose of getting information from the person interviewed, it is sometimes desirable for the interviewer to repeat the answer he has received to a question.
    For the interviewer to rephrase such an answer in his own words is good practice MAINLY because it
    A. gives the interviewer time to make up his next question
    B. gives the person interviewed a chance to correct any possible misunderstanding
    C. gives the person interviewed the feeling that the interviewer considers his answer important
    D. prevents the person interviewed from changing his answer

15.____

16. There are several methods of formulating questions during an interview. The particular method used should be adapted to the interview problems presented by the person being questioned.
    Of the following methods of formulating questions during an interview, the ACCEPTABLE one is for the interviewer to ask questions which
    A. incorporate several items in order to allow a cooperative interviewee freedom to organize his statements
    B. are ambiguous in order to foil a distrustful interviewee
    C. suggest the correct answer in order to assist an interviewee who appears confused
    D. would help an otherwise unresponsive interviewee to become more responsive

16._____

17. For an interviewer to permit the person being interviewed to read the data the interviewer writes as he records the person's responses on a routine departmental form is
    A. *desirable*, because it serves to assure the person interviewed that his responses are being recorded accurately
    B. *undesirable*, because it prevents the interviewer from clarifying uncertain points by asking additional questions
    C. *desirable*, because it makes the time that the person interviewed must wait while the answer is written seem shorter
    D. *undesirable*, because it destroys the confidentiality of the interview

17._____

18. Of the following methods of conducting an interview, the BEST is to
    A. ask questions with "yes" or "no" answers
    B. listen carefully and ask only questions that are pertinent
    C. fire questions at the interviewee so that he must answer sincerely and briefly
    D. read standardized questions to the person being interviewed

18._____

KEY (CORRECT ANSWERS)

1.	A	11.	C
2.	B	12.	B
3.	D	13.	C
4.	B	14.	D
5.	A	15.	B
6.	B	16.	D
7.	D	17.	A
8.	C	18.	B
9.	C		
10.	A		

EXAMINATION SECTION
TEST 1

DIRECTIONS: Each question or incomplete statement is followed by several suggested answers or completions. Select the one that BEST answers the question or completes the statement. *PRINT THE LETTER OF THE CORRECT ANSWER IN THE SPACE AT THE RIGHT.*

Questions 1-5.

DIRECTIONS: Questions 1 through 5 consist of a sentence with an underlined word. For each question, select the choice that is CLOSEST in meaning to the underlined word.

EXAMPLE
This division reviews the fiscal reports of the agency.
In this sentence, the word *fiscal* means MOST NEARLY
    A. financial   B. critical   C. basic   D. personnel
The correct answer is A. "financial" because "financial" is closest to *fiscal*. Therefore, the answer is A.

1. Every good office worker needs basic skills.
   The word *basic* in this sentence means
       A. fundamental   B. advanced   C. unusual   D. outstanding

2. He turned out to be a good instructor.
   The word *instructor* in this sentence means
       A. student   B. worker   C. typist   D. teacher

3. The quantity of work in the office was under study.
   In this sentence, the word *quantity* means
       A. amount   B. flow   C. supervision   D. type

4. The morning was spent examining the time records.
   In this sentence, the word *examining* means
       A. distributing   B. collecting   C. checking   D. filing

5. The candidate filled in the proper spaces on the form.
   In this sentence, the word *proper* means
       A. blank   B. appropriate   C. many   D. remaining

Questions 6-8.

DIRECTIONS: Questions 6 through 8 are to be answered SOLELY on the basis of the information contained in the following paragraph.

The increase in the number of public documents in the last two centuries closely matches the increase in population in the United States. The great number of public documents has become a serious threat to their usefulness. It is necessary to have programs which will reduce the number of public documents that are kept and which will, at the same time, assure keeping those that have value. Such programs need a great deal of thought to have any success.

6. According to the above paragraph, public documents may be less useful if   6.____
   A. the files are open to the public
   B. the record room is too small
   C. the copying machine is operated only during normal working hours
   D. too many records are being kept

7. According to the above paragraph, the growth of the population in the United   7.____
   States has matched the growth in the quantity of public documents for a period of MOST NEARLY _____ years.
   A. 50   B. 100   C. 200   D. 300

8. According to the above paragraph, the increased number of public documents   8.____
   has made it necessary to
   A. find out which public documents are worth keeping
   B. reduce the great number of public documents by decreasing government services
   C. eliminate the copying of all original public documents
   D. avoid all new copying devices

Questions 9-10.

DIRECTIONS: Questions 9 and 10 are to be answered SOLELY on the basis of the information contained in the following paragraph.

The work goals of an agency can best be reached if the employees understand and agree with these goals. One way to gain such understanding and agreement is for management to encourage and seriously consider suggestions from employees in the setting of agency goals.

9. On the basis of the above paragraph, the BEST way to achieve the work goals   9.____
   of an agency is to
   A. make certain that employees work as hard as possible
   B. study the organizational structure of the agency
   C. encourage employees to think seriously about the agency's problems
   D. stimulate employee understanding of the work goals

10. On the basis of the above paragraph, understanding and agreement with agency goals can be gained by   10.____
    A. allowing the employees to set agency goals
    B. reaching agency goals quickly
    C. legislative review of agency operations
    D. employee participation in setting agency goals

Questions 11-15.

DIRECTIONS: Each of Questions 11 through 15 consists of a group of four words. One word in each group is incorrectly spelled. For each question, print the letter of the correct answer in the space at the right that is the same as the letter next to the word which is INCORRECTLY spelled.

EXAMPLE

    A. housing   B. certain   C. budgit   D. money

The word "budgit" is incorrectly spelled, because the correct spelling should be "budget." Therefore, the correct answer is C.

11. A. sentince   B. bulletin   C. notice   D. definition   11.____

12. A. appointment   B. exactly   C. typest   D. light   12.____

13. A. penalty   B. suparvise   C. consider   D. division   13.____

14. A. schedule   B. accurate   C. corect   D. simple   14.____

15. A. suggestion   B. installed   C. proper   D. agincy   15.____

Questions 16-20.

DIRECTIONS: Each Question 16 through 20 consists of a sentence which may be
    A. incorrect because of bad word usage, or
    B. incorrect because of bad punctuation, or
    C. incorrect because of bad spelling, or
    D. correct
Read each sentence carefully. Then print in the space at the right A, B, C, or D, according to the answer you choose from the four choices listed above.
There is only one type of error in each incorrect sentence. If there is no error, the sentence is correct.

EXAMPLE

George Washington was the father of his contry.
This sentence is incorrect because of bad spelling ("contry" instead of "country").
Therefore, the answer is C.

16. The assignment was completed in record time but the payroll for it has not yet 16.____
    been preparid.

17. The operator, on the other hand, is willing to learn me how to use the 17.____
    mimeograph.

18. She is the prettiest of the three sisters. 18.____

19. She doesn't know; if the mail has arrived. 19.____

20. The doorknob of the office door is broke. 20.____

21. A clerk can process a form in 15 minutes. 21.____
    How many forms can that clerk process in six hours?
       A. 10   B. 21   C. 24   D. 90

22. An office staff consists of 120 people. Sixty of them have been assigned to a 22.____
    special project. Of the remaining staff, 20 answer the mail, 10 handle phone
    calls, and the rest operate the office machines.
    The number of people operating the office machines is
       A. 20   B. 30   C. 40   D. 45

23. An office worker received 65 applications but on the first day had to return 23.____
    26 of them for being incomplete and on the second day 25 had to be returned
    for being incomplete.
    How many applications did NOT have to be returned?
       A. 10   B. 12   C. 14   D. 16

24. An office worker answered 63 phone calls in one day and 91 phone calls the 24.____
    next day.
    For these 2 days, what was the average number of phone calls he answered
    per day?
       A. 77   B. 28   C. 82   D. 93

25. An office worker processed 12 vouchers of $8.50 each, 3 vouchers of $3.68 25.____
    each, and 2 vouchers of $1.29 each.
    The TOTAL dollar amount of these vouchers is
       A. $116.04   B. $117.52   C. $118.62   D. $119.04

KEY (CORRECT ANSWERS)

1.	A	11.	A
2.	D	12.	C
3.	A	13.	B
4.	C	14.	C
5.	B	15.	D
6.	D	16.	C
7.	C	17.	A
8.	A	18.	D
9.	D	19.	B
10.	D	20.	A

21. C
22. B
23. C
24. A
25. C

TEST 2

DIRECTIONS: Each question or incomplete statement is followed by several suggested answers or completions. Select the one that BEST answers the question or completes the statement. *PRINT THE LETTER OF THE CORRECT ANSWER IN THE SPACE AT THE RIGHT.*

Questions 1-5.

DIRECTIONS: Each Question from 1 through 5 lists four names. The names may not be exactly the same. Compare the names in each question and mark your answer
- A if all the names are different
- B if only two names are exactly the same
- C if only three names are exactly the same
- D if all four names are exactly the same

EXAMPLE
Jensen, Alfred E.
Jensen, Alfred E.
Jensan, Alfred E.
Jensen, Fred E.

Since the name Jensen, Alfred E. appears twice and is exactly the same in both places, the correct answer is B.

1. A. Riviera, Pedro S.　　B. Rivers, Pedro S.
   C. Riviera, Pedro N.　　D. Riviera, Juan S.

2. A. Guider, Albert　　B. Guidar, Albert
   C. Giuder, Alfred　　D. Guider, Albert

3. A. Blum, Rona　　B. Blum, Rona
   C. Blum, Rona　　D. Blum, Rona

4. A. Raugh, John　　B. Raugh, James
   C. Raughe, John　　D. Raugh, John

5. A. Katz, Stanley　　B. Katz, Stanley
   C. Katze, Stanley　　D. Katz, Stanley

Questions 6-10.

DIRECTIONS: Each Question 6 through 10 consists of numbers or letters in Columns I and II. For each question, compare each line of Column I with its corresponding line in Column II and decide how many lines in Column I are EXACTLY the same as their corresponding lines in Column II. In your answer space, mark your answer
- A if only ONE line in Column I is exactly the same as its corresponding line in Column II
- B if only TWO lines in Column I are exactly the same as their corresponding lines in Column II

2 (#2)

    C if only THREE lines in Column I are exactly the same as their corresponding lines in Column II
    D if all FOUR lines in Column I are exactly the same as their corresponding lines in Column II

EXAMPLE

Column I	Column II
1776	1776
1865	1865
1945	1945
1976	1978

Only three lines in Column I are exactly the same as their corresponding lines in Column II. Therefore, the correct answer is C.

	Column I	Column II	
6.	5653 8727 ZPSS 4952	5653 8728 ZPSS 9453	6.____
7.	PNJP NJPJ JNPN PNJP	PNPJ NJPJ JNPN PNPJ	7.____
8.	effe uWvw KpGj vmnv	eFfe uWvw KpGg vmnv	8.____
9.	5232 PfrC zssz rwwr	5232 PfrN zzss rwww	9.____
10.	czws cecc thrm lwtz	czws cece thrm lwtz	10.____

Questions 11-15.

DIRECTIONS: Questions 11 through 15 have lines of letters and numbers. Each letter should be matched with its number in accordance with the following table.

Letter	F	R	C	A	W	L	E	N	B	T
Matching Number	0	1	2	3	4	5	6	7	8	9

From the table you can determine that the letter F has the matching number 0 below it, the letter R has the matching number 1 below, etc.

For each question, compare each line of letters and numbers carefully to see if each letter has its correct matching number. If all the letters and numbers are matched correctly in

none of the lines of the question, mark your answer A
only *one* of the lines of the question, mark your answer B
only *two* of the lines of the question, mark your answer C
all three lines of the question, mark your answer D

EXAMPLE

WBCR	4826
TLBF	9580
ATNE	3986

There is a mistake in the first line because the letter R should have its matching number 1 instead of the number 6.

The second line is correct because each letter shown has the correct matching number.

There is a mistake in the third line because the letter N should have the matching number 7 instead of the number 8.

Since all the letters and numbers are correct matched in only one of the lines in the sample, the correct answer is B.

11. EBCT   6829   11._____
     ATWR   3961
     NLBW   7584

12. RNCT   1729   12._____
     LNCR   5728
     WAEB   5368

13. NTWB   7948   13._____
     RABL   1385
     TAEF   9360

14. LWRB   5417   14._____
     RLWN   1647
     CBWA   2843

15. ABTC   3792   15._____
     WCER   5261
     AWCN   3417

16. Your job often brings you into contact with the public.   16._____
    Of the following, it would be MOST desirable to explain the reasons for official actions to people coming into your office for assistance because such explanations
    A. help build greater understanding between the public and your agency
    B. help build greater self-confidence in city employees
    C. convince the public that nothing they do can upset a city employee
    D. show the public that city employees are intelligent

17. Assume that you strongly dislike one of your co-workers.
    You should FIRST
    A. discuss your feeling with the co-worker
    B. demand a transfer to another office
    C. suggest to your supervisor that the co-worker should be observed carefully
    D. try to figure out the reason for this dislike before you say or do anything

18. An office worker who has problems accepting authority is MOST likely to find it difficult to
    A. obey rules
    B. understand people
    C. assist other employees
    D. follow complex instructions

19. The employees in your office have taken a dislike to one person and frequently annoy her.
    Your supervisor should
    A. transfer this person to another unit at the first opportunity
    B. try to find out the reason for the staff's attitude before doing anything about it
    C. threaten to transfer the first person observed bothering this person
    D. ignore the situation

20. Assume that your supervisor has asked a worker in your office to get a copy of a report out of the files. You notice the worker as accidentally pulled out the wrong report.
    Of the following, the BEST way for you to handle this situation is to tell
    A. the worker about all the difficulties that will result from this error
    B. the worker about her mistake in a nice way
    C. the worker to ignore this error
    D. your supervisor that this worker needs more training in how to use the files

21. Filing systems differ in their efficiency.
    Which of the following is the BEST way to evaluate the efficiency of a filing system? A
    A. number of times used per day
    B. amount of material that is received each day for filing
    C. amount of time it takes to locate material
    D. type of locking system used

22. In planning ahead so that a sufficient amount of general office supplies is always available, it would be LEAST important to find out the
    A. current office supply needs of the staff
    B. amount of office supplies used last year
    C. days and times that office supplies can be ordered
    D. agency goals and objectives

23. The MAIN reason for establishing routine office work procedures is that once a routine is established
    A. work need not be checked for accuracy
    B. all steps in the routine will take an equal amount of time to perform
    C. each time the job is repeated, it will take less time to perform
    D. each step in the routine will not have to be planned all over again each time

23._____

24. When an office machine centrally located in an agency must be shut down for repairs, the bureaus and divisions using this machine should be informed of the
    A. expected length of time before the machine will be in operation again
    B. estimated cost of repairs
    C. efforts being made to avoid future repairs
    D. type of new equipment which the agency may buy in the future to replace the machine being repaired

24._____

25. If the day's work is properly scheduled, the MOST important result would be that the
    A. supervisor will not have to do much supervision
    B. employee will know what to do next
    C. employee will show greater initiative
    D. job will become routine

25._____

KEY (CORRECT ANSWERS)

1.	A	11.	C
2.	B	12.	B
3.	D	13.	D
4.	B	14.	B
5.	C	15.	A
6.	B	16.	A
7.	B	17.	D
8.	B	18.	A
9.	A	19.	B
10.	C	20.	B

21.	C
22.	D
23.	D
24.	A
25.	B

REPORT WRITING
EXAMINATION SECTION
TEST 1

DIRECTIONS: Each question or incomplete statement is followed by several suggested answers or completions. Select the one that BEST answers the question or completes the statement. *PRINT THE LETTER OF THE CORRECT ANSWER IN THE SPACE AT THE RIGHT.*

Questions 1-3.

DIRECTIONS: Questions 1 to 3 are based on the following example of a report. The report consists of ten numbered sentences, some of which are *not* consistent with the principles of good report writing.

(1) On the evening of February 24, Roscoe and Leroy, two members of the "Red Devils," were entering with a bottle of wine in their hands. (2) It was unusually good wine for these boys to buy, (3) I told them to give me the bottle and they refused, and added that they wouldn't let anyone "put them out." (4) I told them they were entitled to have a good time, but they could not do it the way they wanted; there were certain rules they had to observe. (5) At this point, Roscoe said he had seen me box at camp and suggested that Leroy not accept my offer. (6) Then I said firmly that the admission fee did not give them the authority to tell me what to do. (7) I also told them that, if they thought I would fight them over such a matter, they were sadly mistaken. (8) I added, however, that we could go to the gym right now and settle it another way if they wished. (9) Leroy immediately said that he was sorry, he had not understood the rules, and he did not want his quarter back. (10) On the other hand, they would not give up their bottle either, so they left the premises.

1. Only material that is relevant to the main thought of a report should be included. Which of the following sentences from the report contains material which is LEAST relevant to this report? Sentence
   "A. 2   B. 3   C. 8   D. 9

2. A good report should be arranged in logical order. Which of the following sentences from the report does NOT appear in its proper sequence in the report? Sentence
   A. 3   B. 5   C. 7   D. 9

3. Reports should include all essential information. Of the following, the MOST important fact that is *missing* from this report is:
   A. Who was involved in the incident   B. How the incident was resolved
   C. When the incident took place   D. Where the incident took place

4. The MOST serious of the following faults *commonly* found in explanatory reports is
   A. the use of slang terms   B. excessive details
   C. personal bias   D. redundancy

1._____

2._____

3._____

4._____

5. In reviewing a report he has prepared to submit to his superiors, a supervisor finds that his paragraphs are a typewritten page long and decides to make some revisions.
Of the following, the MOST important question he should ask about each paragraph is
   A. Are the words too lengthy?
   B. Is the idea under discussion too abstract?
   C. Is more than one central thought being expressed?
   D. Are the sentences too long?

5._____

6. The summary or findings of a long management report intended for the typical manager should, *generally*, appear _____ the report.
   A. at the very beginning of
   B. at the end of
   C. throughout
   D. in the middle of

6._____

7. In preparing a report that includes several tables, if not otherwise instructed, the typist should MOST properly include a list of tables
   A. in the introductory part of the report
   B. at the end of each chapter in the body of the report
   C. in the supplementary part of the report as an appendix
   D. in the supplementary part of the report as a part of the index

7._____

8. When typing a preliminary draft of a report, the one of the following which you should *generally* NOT do is to
   A. erase typing errors and deletions rather than "X"ing them out
   B. leave plenty of room at the top, bottom, and sides of each page
   C. make only the number of copies that you are asked to make
   D. type double or triple space

8._____

9. When you determine the methods of emphasis you will use in typing the titles, headings and subheadings of a report, the one of the following which it is MOST important to keep in mind is that
   A. all headings of the same rank should be typed in the same way
   B. all headings should be typed in the single style which is most pleasing to the eye
   C. headings should not take up more than one-third of the page width
   D. only one method should be used for all headings, whatever their rank

9._____

10. The one of the following ways in which inter-office memoranda *differ* from long formal reports is that they, *generally*,
    A. are written as if the reader is familiar with the vocabulary and technical background of the writer
    B. do not have a "subject line" which describes the major topic covered in the text
    C. include a listing of reference materials which support the memo writer's conclusions
    D. require that a letter of transmittal be attached

10._____

11. It is *preferable* to print information on a field report rather than write it out longhand MAINLY because
    A. printing takes less time to write than writing long hand
    B. printing is usually easier to read than longhand writing
    C. longhand writing on field reports is not acceptable in court cases
    D. printing occupies less space on a report than longhand writing

11.____

12. Of the following characteristics of a written report, the one that is MOST important is its
    A. length   B. accuracy   C. organization   D. grammar

12.____

13. A written report to your superior contains many spelling errors.
    Of the following statements relating to spelling errors, the one that is MOST NEARLY correct is that
    A. this is unimportant as long as the meaning of the report is clear
    B. readers of the report will ignore the many spelling errors
    C. readers of the report will get a poor opinion of the writer of the report
    D. spelling errors are unimportant as long as the grammar is correct

13.____

14. Written reports to your superior should have the same general arrangement and layout.
    The BEST reason for this requirement is that the
    A. report will be more accurate
    B. report will be more complete
    C. person who reads the report will know what the subject of the report is
    D. person who reads the report will know where to look for information in the report

14.____

15. The first paragraph of a report usually contains detailed information on the subject of the report.
    Of the following, the BEST reason for this requirement is to enable the
    A. reader to quickly find the subject of the report
    B. typist to immediately determine the subject of the report so that she will understand what she is typing
    C. clerk to determine to whom copies of the report will be needed
    D. typist to quickly determine how many copies of the report will be needed

15.____

16. Of the following statements concerning reports, the one which is LEAST valid is:
    A. A case report should contain factual material to support conclusions made
    B. An extremely detailed report may be of less value than a brief report giving the essential facts
    C. Highly technical language should be avoided as far as possible in preparing a report to be used at a court trial
    D. The position of the important facts in a report does not influence the emphasis placed on them by the reader

16.____

17. Suppose that you realize that you have made an error in a report that has been forwarded to another unit. You know that this error is not likely to be discovered for some time.
    Of the following, the MOST advisable course of action for you to take is to
    A. approach the supervisor of the other unit on an informal basis, and ask him to correct the error
    B. say nothing about it since most likely one error will not invalidate the entire report
    C. tell your supervisor immediately that you have made an error so that it may be corrected, if necessary
    D. wait until the error is discovered and then admit that you had made it

17.____

18. In a report, words in a sentence must be arranged properly to make sure that the intended meaning of the sentence is clear.
    The sentence below that does NOT make sense because a clause has been separated from the word on which its meaning depends is:
    A. To be a good writer, clarity is necessary.
    B. To be a good writer, you must write clearly.
    C. You must write clearly to be a good writer.
    D. Clarity is necessary to good writing.

18.____

19. The use of a graph to show statistical data in a report is *superior* to a table because it
    A. emphasizes approximations
    B. emphasizes facts and relationships more dramatically
    C. presents data more accurately
    D. is easily understood by the average reader

19.____

20. Of the following, the degree of formality required of a written report is, MOST likely to depend on the
    A. subject matter of the report
    B. frequency of its occurrence
    C. amount of time available for its preparation
    D. audience for whom the report is intended

20.____

Questions 21-25.

DIRECTIONS: Questions 21 through 25 consist of sets of four sentences lettered A, B, C, and D. For each question, choose the sentence which is grammatically and stylistically MOST appropriate for use in a formal written report.

21. A. It is recommended, therefore, that the impasse panel hearings are to be convened on September 30.
    B. It is therefore recommended that the impasse panel hearings be convened on September 30.
    C. Therefore, it is recommended to convene the impasse panel hearings on September 30.
    D. It is recommended that the impasse panel hearings therefore should be convened on September 30.

21.____

22. A. Penalties have been assessed for violating the Taylor Law by several unions.
    B. When they violated provisions of the Taylor Law, several unions were later penalized.
    C. Several unions have been penalized for violating provisions of the Taylor Law.
    D. Several unions' violating provisions of the Taylor Law resulted in them being penalized.

    22._____

23. A. The number of disputes settled through mediation has increased significantly over the past two years.
    B. The number of disputes settled through mediation are increasing significantly over two-year periods.
    C. Over the past two years, through mediation, the number of disputes settled increased significantly.
    D. There is a significant increase over the past two years of the number of disputes settled through mediation.

    23._____

24. A. The union members will vote to determine if the contract is to be approved.
    B. It is not yet known whether the union members will ratify the proposed contract.
    C. When the union members vote, that will determine the new contract.
    D. Whether the union members will ratify the proposed contract, it is not yet known.

    24._____

25. A. The parties agreed to an increase in fringe benefits in return for greater work productivity.
    B. Greater productivity was agreed to be provided in return for increased fringe benefits.
    C. Productivity and fringe benefits are interrelated; the higher the former, the more the latter grows.
    D. The contract now provides that the amount of fringe benefits will depend upon the level of output by the workers.

    25._____

KEY (CORRECT ANSWERS)

1.	A	11.	B
2.	B	12.	B
3.	D	13.	C
4.	C	14.	D
5.	C	15.	A
6.	A	16.	D
7.	A	17.	C
8.	A	18.	A
9.	A	19.	B
10.	A	20.	D

21. B
22. C
23. A
24. B
25. A

TEST 2

DIRECTIONS: Each question or incomplete statement is followed by several suggested answers or completions. Select the one that BEST answers the question or completes the statement. *PRINT THE LETTER OF THE CORRECT ANSWER IN THE SPACE AT THE RIGHT.*

Questions 1-4.

DIRECTIONS: Questions 1 through 4 are to be answered on the basis of the following report which was prepared by a supervisor for inclusion in his agency's annual report.

Line #

1   On Oct. 13, I was assigned to study the salaries paid
2   to clerical employees in various titles by the city and by
3   private industry in the area.
4   In order to get the data I needed, I called Mr. Johnson at
5   the Bureau of the Budget and the payroll officers at X Corp.-
6   a brokerage house, Y Co. –an insurance company, and Z Inc. –
7   a publishing firm. None of them was available and I had to call
8   all of them again the next day.
9   When I finally got the information I needed, I drew up a
10 chart, which is attached. Note that not all of the companies I
11 contacted employed people at all the different levels used in the
12 city service.
13 The conclusions I draw from analyzing this information is
14 as follows: The city's entry-level salary is about average for
15 the region; middle-level salaries are generally higher in the
16 city government than in private industry; but salaries at the
17 highest levels in private industry are better than city em-
18 ployees' pay.

1. Which of the following criticisms about the style in which this report is written is MOST valid?
    A. It is too informal.
    B. It is too concise.
    C. It is too choppy.
    D. The syntax is too complex.

    1.____

2. Judging from the statements made in the report, the method followed by this employee in performing his research was
    A. *good*; he contacted a representative sample of businesses in the area
    B. *poor*; he should have drawn more definite conclusions
    C. *good*; he was persistent in collecting information
    D. *poor*; he did not make a thorough study

    2.____

3. One sentence in this report contains a grammatical error. This sentence *begins* on line number
    A. 4   B. 7   C. 10   D. 13

    3.____

4. The type of information given in this report which should be presented in footnotes or in an appendix, is the
   A. purpose of the study
   B. specifics about the businesses contacted
   C. reference to the chart
   D. conclusions drawn by the author

4.____

5. Of the following, a DISTINGUISHING characteristic of a written report intended for the head of your agency as compared to a report prepared for a lower-echilon staff member is that the report for the agency head should, *usually*, include
   A. considerably more detail, especially statistical data
   B. the essential details in an abbreviated form
   C. all available source material
   D. an annotated bibliography

5.____

6. Assume that you are asked to write a lengthy report for use by the administrator of your agency, the subject of which is "The Impact of Proposed New Data Processing Operations on Line Personnel" in your agency. You decide that the *most* appropriate type of report for you to prepare is an analytical report, including recommendations.
   The MAIN reason for your decision is that
   A. the subject of the report is extremely complex
   B. large sums of money are involved
   C. the report is being prepared for the administrator
   D. you intend to include charts and graphs

6.____

7. Assume that you are preparing a report based on a survey dealing with the attitudes of employees in Division X regarding proposed new changes in compensating employees for working overtime. Three percent of the respondents to the survey voluntarily offer an unfavorable opinion on the method of assigning overtime work, a question not specifically asked of the employees. On the basis of this information, the MOST appropriate and significant of the following comments for you to make in the report with regard to employees' attitudes on assigning overtime work is that
   A. an insignificant percentage of employees dislike the method of assigning overtime work
   B. three percent of the employees in Division X dislike the method of assigning overtime work
   C. three percent of the sample selected for the survey voiced an unfavorable opinion on the method of assigning overtime work
   D. some employees voluntarily voiced negative feelings about the method of assigning overtime work, making it impossible to determine the extent of this attitude

7.____

8. Assume that you have been asked to prepare a narrative summary of the monthly reports submitted by employees in your division.
   In preparing your summary of this month's reports, the FIRST step to take is to
   A. read through the reports, noting their general content and any unusual features
   B. decide how many typewritten pages your summary should contain
   C. make a written summary of each separate report, so that you will not have to go back to the original reports again
   D. ask each employee which points he would prefer to see emphasized in your summary

9. Assume that an administrative officer is writing a brief report to his superior outlining the advantages of matrix organization.
   Of the following, it would be INCORRECT to state that
   A. in matrix organization, a project is emphasized by designating one individual as the focal point for all matters pertaining to it
   B. utilization of manpower can be flexible in matrix organization because reservoir of specialists is maintained in the line operations
   C. the usual line-staff management is generally reversed in matrix organization
   D. in matrix organization, responsiveness to project needs is generally faster due to establishing needed communication lines and decision points

10. Written reports dealing with inspections of work and installations SHOULD be
    A. as long and detailed as practicable
    B. phrased with personal interpretations
    C. limited to the important facts of the inspection
    D. technically phrased to create an impression on superiors

11. It is important to use definite, exact words in preparing a descriptive report and to avoid, as much as possible, nouns that have vague meanings and, possibly, a different meaning for the reader than for the author.
    Which of the following sentences contains only nouns that are *definite* and *exact*?
    A. The free enterprise system should be vigorously encouraged in the United States.
    B. Arley Swopes climbed Mount Everest three times last year.
    C. Beauty is a characteristic of all the women at the party.
    D. Gil Noble asserts that he is a real democrat.

12. One way of shortening n unnecessarily long report is to reduce sentence length by eliminating the use of several words where a single one that does not alter the meaning will do.
    Which of the following sentences CANNOT be shortened without losing some of its information content?
    A. After being polished, the steel ball bearings ran at maximum speed.
    B. After the close of the war, John Taylor was made the recipient of a pension.
    C. In this day and age, you can call anyone up on the telephone.
    D. She is attractive in appearance, but she is a rather selfish person.

13. Employees are required to submit written reports of all unusual occurrences promptly.
    The BEST reason for such promptness is that the
    A. report may be too long if made at one's convenience
    C. report will tend to be more accurate as to facts
    D. employee is likely to make a better report under pressure

14. In making a report, it is poor practice to erase information on the report in order to make a change because
    A. there may be a question of what was changed and why it was changed
    B. you are likely to erase through the paper and tear the report
    C. the report will no longer look neat and presentable
    D. the duplicate copies will be smudged

15. The one of the following which BEST describes a periodic report is that it
    A. provides a record of accomplishments for a given time span and a comparison with similar time spans in the past
    B. covers the progress made in a project that has been postponed
    C. integrates, summarizes, and, perhaps, interprets published data on technical or scientific material
    D. describes a decision, advocates a policy or action, and presents facts in support of the writer's position

16. The PRIMARY purpose of including pictorial illustrations in a formal report is *usually* to
    A. amplify information which has been adequately treated verbally
    B. present details that are difficult to describe verbally
    C. provide the reader with a pleasant, momentary distraction
    D. present supplementary information incidental to the main ideas developed in the report

KEY (CORRECT ANSWERS)

1.	A		6.	A
2.	D		7.	D
3.	D		8.	A
4.	B		9.	C
5.	B		10.	C

11.	B.
12.	A.
13.	C
14.	A.
15.	A.
16	B.

ARITHMETICAL REASONING
EXAMINATION SECTION
TEST 1

DIRECTIONS: Each question or incomplete statement is followed by several suggested answers or completions. Select the one that BEST answers the question or completes the statement. *PRINT THE LETTER OF THE CORRECT ANSWER IN THE SPACE AT THE RIGHT.*

1. On January 1, a family was receiving supplementary monthly public assistance of $280 for food, $240 for rent, and $140 for other necessities. In the spring, their rent rose by 10%, and their rent allotment was adjusted accordingly. In the summer, due to the death of a family member, their allotments for food and other necessities were reduced by 1/7.
   Their monthly allowance check in the fall should be
   A. $623   B. $644   C. $664   D. $684

   1.____

2. Twice a month, a certain family receives a $340 general allowance for rent, food, and clothing expense. In addition, the family receives a specific supplementary allotment for utilities of $384 a year, which is added to their semi-monthly check.
   If the general allowance alone is reduced by 5%, what will be the TOTAL amount of their next semi-monthly check?
   A. $323   B. $339   C. $340   D. $355

   2.____

3. If each supervising clerk in a certain unit sees an average of 9 clients in a 7-hour day and there are 15 supervising clerks in the unit, APPROXIMATELY how many clients will be seen in a 35-hour week?
   A. 315   B. 405   C. 675   D. 945

   3.____

4. In one day, an aide receives 18 inquiries by phone and 27 inquiries in person. What percentage of the inquiries received that day were by phone?
   A. 33%   B. 40%   C. 45%   D. 60%

   4.____

5. If the weekly paychecks for 5 employees are $258.64, $325.48, $287.50, and $313.12, then the combined weekly income for the 5 employee is
   A. $1,455.68   B. $1,456.08   C. $1,462.68   D. $1,474.08

   5.____

6. Suppose that there are 17 aides working in an office where many community complaints are received by telephone. In one ten-day period, 4,250 calls were received.
   If the same number of calls were received each day and the aides divided the work load equally, about how many calls did each aide respond to daily?
   A. 25   B. 35   C. 75   D. 250

   6.____

7. Suppose that an assignment was divided among 5 aides.
If the first aide spent 67 hours on the assignment, the second aide spent 95 hours, the third aide spent 52 hours, the fourth aide spent 78 hours, and the fifth aide spent 103 hours, what was the AVERAGE amount of time spent by each aide on the assignment? _____ hours.
   A. 71   B. 75   C. 79   D. 83

8. If there are 240 employees in a center and 1/3 are absent on the day of a bad snowstorm, how many employees were at work in the center on that day?
   A. 80   B. 120   C. 160   D. 200

9. Suppose that an aide takes 25 minutes to prepare a letter to a client.
If the aide is assigned to prepare 9 letters on a certain day, how much time should be set aside for this task? _____ hours.
   A. 3¾   B. 4¼   C. 4¾   D. 5¼

10. Suppose that a certain center uses both Form A and Form B in the course of its daily work and that Form A is used 4 times as often as Form B.
If the total number of both forms used in one week is 750, how many times was Form A used?
    A. 100   B. 200   C. 400   D. 600

11. Suppose a center has a budget of $2,185.40 from which 8 desks costing $156.10 apiece must be bought.
How many additional desks can be ordered from this budget after the 8 desks have been purchased?
    A. 4   B. 6   C. 9   D. 14

12. When researching a particular case, a team of 16 aides was asked to check through 234 folders to obtain the necessary information.
If half the aides worked twice as fast as the other half, and the slow group checked through 12 folders each hour, about how long would it take to complete the assignment? _____ hours.
    A. 4¼   B. 5   C. 6   D. 6½

13. The difference in the cost of two typewriters is $56.64.
If the less expensive typewriter costs $307.22, what is the cost of the other typewriter?
    A. $343.86   B. $344.06   C. $363.86   D. $364.06

14. At the start of a year, a family was receiving a public assistance grant of $382 twice a month, on the first and fifteenth of each month. On March 1, their rent allowance was decreased from $150 to $142 a month since they had moved to a smaller apartment. On August 1 their semi-monthly food allowance, which had been $80.40, was raised by 10%.
In that year, the TOTAL amount of money disbursed to this family was
    A. $4,544.20   B. $6,581.40   C. $9,088.40   D. $9,168.40

15. It is discovered that a client has received double public assistance for 2 months by having been enrolled at two service centers of the Department of Social Services. The client should have received $168 twice a month instead of the double amount. He now agrees to repay the money by equal deductions from his public assistance check over a period of 12 months.
What will the amount of his NEXT check be?
    A. $112   B. $140   C. $154   D. $160

16. Suppose a study is being made of the composition of 3,550 families receiving public assistance. Of the first 1,050 families reviewed, 18% had four or more children.
If, in the remaining number of families, the percentage with four or more children is half as high as the percentage in the group already reviewed, then the percentage of families with four or more children in the entire group of families is MOST NEARLY
    A. 12   B. 14   C. 16   D. 17

17. Suppose that food prices have risen 13%, and an increase of the same amount has been granted in the food allotment given to people receiving public assistance.
If a family has been receiving $810 a month, 35% of which is allotted for food, then the TOTAL amount of public assistance this family receives per month will be changed to
    A. $805.42   B. $840.06   C. $846.86   D. $899.42

18. Assume that the food allowance is to be raised 5% in August but will be retroactive for four months to April. .
The retroactive allowance is to be divided into equal sections and added to the public assistance checks for August, September, October, November, and December.
A family which has been receiving $840 monthly, 40% of which was allotted for food, will receive what size check in August?
    A. $853.44   B. $856.80   C. $861.00   D. $870.24

19. A blind client, who receives $210 public assistance twice a month, inherits 14 shares of stock worth $180 each. The client is required to sell the stock and spend his inheritance before receiving more public assistance.
Using his public assistance allowance as a guide, how many months are his new assets expected to last?
    A. 6   B. 7   C. 8   D. 12

20. The Department of Social Services has 16 service centers. These centers may be divided into those which are downtown and those which are uptown. Two of the centers are special service centers and are downtown, while the remainder of the centers are general service centers. There is a total of 7 service centers downtown.
The percentage of the general service centers which are uptown is MOST NEARLY
    A. 56   B. 64   C. 69   D. 79

21. For six months, a family lived in a 4-room apartment where they paid $380 a month. They made an intrasite move to a 4-room apartment where they paid $85 per room a month for six months.
Comparing the two six-month periods, the TOTAL amount of money the family saved by making the intrasite was
A. $240   B. $290   C. $430   D. $590

22. To calculate a tenant's usable income, you should make Social Security deductions of 4.4 percent on salary up to a maximum of $9,000 and State Disability deductions of .5 percent on salary up to $3,000.
What does a tenant's combined deduction amount to if his annual salary is $13,400?
A. $411.00   B. $568.60   C. $619.60   D. $700.00

23. If the temporary relocation expenses for housing are set at $18 per day for one adult and $10 per day for each additional person in a room, how much money is allowed for a woman and four children temporarily relocated in one room for a period of six days?
A. $168   B. $348   C. $378   D. $518

24. According to relocation policy, a family relocating to private housing from federally-aided or certain other sites will be granted a relocation payment. This payment equals the difference between 1/5 of the family's yearly income and the scheduled yearly rent for a standard apartment for their size family.
Suppose a 2-person family whose yearly income is $12,900 has been unable to obtain public housing and so finds a one-bedroom private apartment. The scheduled rent for a one-bedroom apartment appropriate for their occupancy is $240 a month.
What payment will they receive?
A. $240   B. $288   C. $300   D. $410

25. A family on a housing relocation site is paying $410 per month for rent. This represents 25% of their gross monthly income.
If the husband earns 4/5 of their total combined monthly income, how much does the wife earn per month?
A. $328   B. $540   C. $1,280   D. $1,500

KEY (CORRECT ANSWERS)

1.	A	11.	B
2.	B	12.	D
3.	C	13.	C
4.	B	14.	D
5.	B	15.	B
6.	A	16.	A
7.	C	17.	C
8.	C	18.	D
9.	A	19.	A
10.	D	20.	B

21.	A
22.	A
23.	B
24.	C
25.	A

SOLUTIONS TO PROBLEMS

1. After spring, the rent allotment should be $(240+24) = $264. After the summer, the reduced allotment for food and other necessities should be $[(280+140) − 1/7(280+140)] = $(420-1/7(420)] = $(420-60) = $360. The monthly check in the fall including rent, food, and other necessities should be $360 + $264 = $624.

2. Amount of general allowance in the family's semi-monthly check = $340. Amount of utilities allotment in the family's semi-monthly check: ($\frac{384}{12}$ × ½) = $16. Amount of general allowance in family' semi-monthly check after a 5% reduction = $340 less 5% of $340 = $(340-17) = $3223. Total amount of the next month's semi-monthly check: Reduced general allowance + utilities allotment = $323 + $16 = $339.

3. During 7 hours, a total of (15)(9) = 135 clients can be seen. Thus, in 35 hours, a total of (135)(5) = 675 clients will be seen.

4. 18(18+27) = .40 = 40%

5. $258.64 + $325.48 + $287.34 + $271.50 + $313.12 = $1,456.08

6. 4250/10 = 425 calls per day. Then, 425/17 = 25

7. (67+95+52+78+103)/5 = 79 hours

8. Number present = (240)(2/3) = 160

9. (25)(9) = 225 min. = 3 hrs. 45 min. = 3 ¾ hours

10. Let x, 1/4x = number of forms A, B, respectively. Then, x + 1/4x = 750. Solving, x = 600

11. $2,185.40 − (8)($156.10) = $936.60. Then, $936.60 ÷ $156.10 = 6 desks

12. Since the slow group did 12 folders each hour, the faster group did 24 folders each hour. Then, 234/(12+24) = 6 ½ hrs.

13. Expensive typewriter costs $307.22 + $56.64 = $363.86

14. For months of January and February, the amount the family receives is $(382×2×2) = $1528
    For months of March through July, the family receives $(764-8) × 5 = $3780
    For months August through December, the family receives $(756+16.08) × 5 = $3860.40
    The total amount of money disbursed to this family is $1528 + $3780 + $3860.40 = $9,168.40

15. The overpayment for 2 months = ($168)(4) = $672. If this is paid back over 12 months, each month's amount is reduced by $672/12 = $56. Then, each check (semi-monthly) is reduced by $28. His next check will be $168 - $28 = $140

7 (#1)

16. $(1050)(.18) + (2500)(.09) = 414$. Then, $414/3550 = 12\%$

17. $(\$810)(.35) = \$283.50$ originally allotted for food. The new food allotment = $(\$283.50)(1.13) = \$320.355$. The total assistance now = $\$810 - \$283.50 + \$320.355 = \$846.855$ or $\$846.86$

18. $(\$840)(.40) = \$336$ per month for food. The new food allowance = $(\$336)(1.05) = \$352.80$ per month. The difference of $16.80 is retroactive to April, which means $(\$16.80)(9) = \$151.20$ additional money for August through December. Each check for these 5 months will be increased by $\$15.20/5 = 30.24$. Thus, the check in August = $\$840 + 30.24 = \$840 + 30.24 = \$870.24$

19. $(\$180)(14) = \$2520$. Then, $\$2520/\$420 = 6$ months

20. 5 general are downtown; 9 of 14 general are uptown; $9/14 \approx 64\%$

21. $(\$85)(4) = \$340$ per month. Savings per month = $\$380 - \$340 = \$40$ For six months, the savings = $\$240$

22. $(\$9000(.044) + (\$3000)(.005) = \$411$ total deductions

23. $(\$18+\$40)(6) = \$348$ relocation expenses

24. $(\$240)(12) - (1/5)(\$12,900) = \$300$ relocation payment

25. $\$410 \div .25 = \$1640$. The wife earns $(1640)(1/5) = \$328$ each month

TEST 2

DIRECTIONS: Each question or incomplete statement is followed by several suggested answers or completions. Select the one that BEST answers the question or completes the statement. *PRINT THE LETTER OF THE CORRECT ANSWER IN THE SPACE AT THE RIGHT.*

1. A project tenant who owns and drives a taxicab for living, reports for a three-month period an income of $6,250 after operating expenses of $1,300 have been considered. In addition, his tips are valued at 12% of his income before operating expenses.
   An estimate of his yearly income is MOST NEARLY
   A. $22,000   B. $23,000   C. $28,000
   D. $28,500   E. $29,000

   1.____

2. The maximum annual subsidy which can be paid by the State toward the operation of any low-rent housing project is the sum of the annual interest on the total original loan or building the project and 1% of the portion of the loan actually spent.
   If the original loan for a project was $8,000,000 at 1¾% interest, but only $7,500,000 was actually spent, then the MAXIMUM annual subsidy is
   A. $140,000   B. $145,000   C. $215,000
   D. $220,000   E. $271,250

   2.____

3. In 2020, the cost of repairs and maintenance at a certain housing project was $5,589 more than in 2019, representing an increase of 4.6%. A further increase at the same rate was anticipated for 2021.
   The cost of repairs and maintenance in 2021 was MOST NEARLY
   A. $127,100
   B. $132,700
   C. $132,900
   D. $133,000
   E. an amount which cannot be determined from the given data

   3.____

4. Each day a delivery truck used by the Housing Authority travels 25 miles from a project to a storehouse and 25 miles on the return trip. It travels at the rate of 30 miles per hour going to the storehouse and at the rate of 20 miles per hour returning.
   The average rate, in miles per hour, for the roundtrip is MOST NEARLY
   A. 24
   B. 25
   C. 26
   D. the square root of 600
   E. an amount which cannot be determined from the given data

   4.____

5. A report on the first 6,000 applications for apartments in a certain project containing 1,400 apartments indicated that those who were ineligible fell into four categories: 2,800 ineligible for reason A, 600 ineligible for reason B, 1,200 ineligible for reason C, and 400 ineligible for reason D.

   5.____

If the same proportions continue for the remaining 21,500 applications, then the percentage of eligible applicants who can be given apartments in the project is MOST NEARLY
A. 25   B. 30   C. 33   D. 40   E. 60

6. The number of applications for apartments in low-rent housing projects was 40,000 in 2019. The number of applications increased 5% in 2020, and increased again in 2021 by 6% over the 2,000 total.
The percentage by which the 2021 figures exceed the 2019 figures is
A. 5.3   B. 6.0   C. 11.0   D. 11.3   E. 30.0

7. A rectangular lot, 75 feet by 11.0 feet, was purchased as part of a project site for $28,500.
The price per square foot of this lot is MOST NEARLY
A. $2.85   B. $3.45   C. $3.95   D. $30.00   E. $30.95

8. It has been estimated that 125 kilowatt-hours of electricity are used each month in one average Housing Authority apartment at a cost of 14.8 cents per kilowatt-hour.
On this basis, the total cost of the electricity used in one year in a project containing 1,400 apartments is MOST NEARLY
A. $20,000   B. $25,000   C. $200,000
D. $250,000   E. $2,000,000

9. The walls and ceilings of 20 rooms are to be painted with the same kind of paint, each room being 15 feet long, 12 feet wide, and 10 feet high. Each room contains two windows, each 3 feet by 6 feet, and a door 3 feet by 8 feet, which are not to be painted. One gallon of paint covers 400 square feet of surface.
The number of gallons of paint needed is MOST NEARLY
A. 33   B. 34   C. 35   D. 36   E. 75

10. A group of buildings is valued at $11,500,000. Assume that the cos of fire insurance for these buildings is 5.3 cents per $100 of valuation per year.
The cost of fire insurance for one year is MOST NEARLY
A. $600   B. $6,000   C. $20,000
D. $60,000   E. $2,000,000

11. Of the 15 employees in a certain unit, one-third earn $27,600 per year, three earn $32,600, one earns $46,400, and the rest earn $33,800.
The average salary of the employees of this unit is MOST NEARLY
A. $31,000   B. $32,000   C. $33,000   D. $34,000   E. $35,000

12. Four pieces, each 2'8½" long, are cut from a piece of pipe 16½' long.
The length of the remaining piece of pipe is
A. 6'8½"   B. 6'10"   C. 6'10⅜"   D. 6'11⅛"   E. 9'9½"

13. A tenant ears E dollars a month, spends S dollars a week, and saves the rest. 13.____
The tenant's yearly savings can be expressed by
    A. 12(E-4S)   B. 12E – 52S   C. 12(E-S)
    D. 52(E-4S)   E. E - S

14. A unit of fifteen Housing Assistants has been assigned the job of interviewing 14.____
applicants. Each interview takes 35 minutes, and an additional 10 minutes is needed for making entries and notes. The last interview each day is always scheduled so that it can be completed that day.
The number of applicants who can be interviewed in a week, consisting of five 7-hour days, is MOST NEARLY
    A. 375   B. 525   C. 675   D. 700   E. 725

15. A review of the 14,000 applications for apartments in a certain project 15.____
containing 1,200 apartments indicated that 4,800 applicants were eligible and 6,400 were ineligible. No decision could be reached on the remaining applications because certain necessary information was omitted by the applicants, but it was assumed that the proportion of eligible and ineligible applicants would remain the same as in those already decided.
On the basis of these figures, the percentage of eligible applicants who can be given apartments in the project is
    A. under 17%   B. 17%   C. 20%
    D. 25%   E. 33 1/3%

16. An oil burner in a housing development burns 76 gallons of fuel oil per hour. 16.____
At 9 A.M. on a very cold day, the superintendent asks the Housing Manager to put in an emergency order for more fuel oil. At that time, he reports that he has on hand 266 gallons. At noon, he again comes to the manager, notifying him that no oil has been delivered.
The MAXIMUM amount of time that he can continue to furnish heat without receiving more oil is
    A. no more time   B. ½ hour   C. 1 hour
    D. 1½ hours   E. 2 hours

17. As a result of reports received by the Housing Authority concerning the reputed 17.____
ineligibility of 756 tenants because of above-standard incomes, an intensive check of their employers has been ordered. Four housing assistants have been assigned to this task. At the end of 6 days at 7 hours each, they have checked on 336 tenants. In order to speed up the investigation, two more housing assistants are assigned to this point.
If they worked at the same rate, the number of additional 7-hour days it would take to complete the job is MOST NEARLY
    A. 1   B. 3   C. 5   D. 7   E. 9

4 (#2)

18. A municipal aide on a special trip is returning to his office from a point 17½ miles away, and makes the return trip to his office at an average speed of 25 miles an hour, except for a 15-minute stopover at one point to get a flat tire fixed. The time it should take him to reach his office is MOST NEARLY _____ minutes.
    A. 12   B. 22   C. 36   D. 42   E. 57

18._____

19. A district office has an assigned staff of 320 employees. Of this number, 25% are not available for duty due to illness, vacations, and other reasons. Of those who are available for duty, 1/8 are assigned to auditing and special projects, and the rest to handling the workload.
    The ACTUAL number of employees available for handling the workload is
    A. 350   B. 310   C. 270   D. 210   E. 180

19._____

20. Two dozen shuttlecocks and four badminton rackets are to be purchased for a playground. The shuttlecocks are priced at $3.60 each, and the rackets at $27.50 each. The playground receives a discount of 30% from these prices.
    The TOTAL cost of this equipment is
    A. $72.90   B. $114.30   C. $137.48   D. $186.00   E. $220.70

20._____

21. On January 1, a family was receiving public assistance allowance of $185 for food, $53 for clothing, $17.50 for utilities, and $22 for personal needs, all semi-monthly, and a monthly allowance of $550 for rent. On May 1, the rent allowance was increased by 12% but all other allowances remained the same for the rest of the year.
    The TOTAL amount of money granted this family during the year was
    A. $10,528   B. $13,262   C. $13,788
    D. $21,056   E. $27,676

21._____

22. It has been decided to make changes in food allotments to clients receiving public assistance to conform to changes in food costs. Of the food allowance, 30% is intended for meat, 30% for fruits and vegetables, 25% for groceries, and 15% for dairy products. Assume that meat prices have gone up 5%, and dairy prices have remained the same.
    For a family that has been receiving $400 per month for food, the new monthly food allowance will be
    A. $333   B. $375   C. $393   D. $403.50   E. $420

22._____

23. On January 1, a family was receiving a public assistance allowance of $195 for food, $63 for clothing, $27.50 for utilities, and $32 for personal needs, all semi-monthly, and a monthly allowance of $510 for rent. On June 1, the rent allowance was increased by 12%, but all other allowances remained the same for the rest of the year.
    The TOTAL amount of money granted this family during the year was
    A. $13,843.40   B. $14,107.20   C. $14,168.40
    D. $14,474.40   E. $16,886.80

23._____

24. A member of a family receiving public assistance amounting to $600 monthly has obtained a part-time job, for which he is paid $40 a day. He is employed 3 days a week. His carfare costs $3.00 per day and his lunches $2.00 per day. Assume that there are $4^1/_3$ weeks per month. The Department of Welfare requires that net earnings be deducted from relief allowances.
The family's semi-monthly public assistance allowances should be reduced to
   A. $40.00   B. $72.50   C. $96.25   D. $123.75   E. $145.00

24.____

25. A couple living in a furnished room has been receiving a public assistance grant of $375 semi-monthly and has been paying a weekly rent of $75. The landlord has been granted a 12% increase in rent. Assume that a month consists of $4^1/_3$ weeks.
The amount of the new semi-monthly grant, including this rent increase, that the couple will receive will be MOST NEARLY
   A. $394.50   B. $397   C. $409   D. $514   E. $557

25.____

KEY (CORRECT ANSWERS)

1.	D		11.	B
2.	C		12.	A
3.	C		13.	B
4.	A		14.	C
5.	B		15.	C
6.	D		16.	B
7.	B		17.	C
8.	D		18.	E
9.	A		19.	D
10.	B		20.	C

21. C
22. C
23. C
24. B
25. A

6 (#2)

SOLUTIONS TO PROBLEMS

1. For 3 months, income = $6,250 + (.12)($7550) = $7156. Then, annual income = ($7154)(4) = $28,624, closest to $28,500.

2. Maximum annual subsidy = ($8,000,000)(.0175) + (.01)($7,500,000) = $215,000

3. Cost in 2019 = $5589/.046 = $121,500. The cost in 2020 = $121,500 + $5589 = $127,089. This means the cost in 2021 = ($127,089)(1.046) = $132,900

4. Average rate = total distance/total time = (25+25) ÷ (25/30 + 25/20) = 24 mph

5. Out of 600, number of eligible = 6000 – 2800 – 600 – 1200 – 400 = 1000. Thus, for 27,500 applications, (1/6)(27,500) = 4583 would be eligible. Finally, 1400 ÷ 4583 ≈ 30%

6. Number of applications in 2020 = (40,000)(1.05) = 42,000. Number of applications in 2021 = (42,000)(1.06) = 44,520. Then, (44,520–40,000) ÷ 40,000 = 11.3%

7. $28,500 ÷ [(75×110)] = $3.45 per sq. ft.

8. Total cost = (125)(.148)(12)(1400) = $310,800; closest to choice D of $250,000

9. Painted area of each room = (2)(15)(10) + (2)(12)(10) + (15)(12) – (2)(3)(6) – (3)(8) = 660 sq. ft. So, (20)(660) = 13,200 sq. ft. to be painted in all rooms. Finally, 13,200/400 = 33 gallons of paint needed

10. Insurance cost = (.053)($11,500,000)/$100 = $6095, closest to $6000

11. [(5)($27,600) + (3)($32,600) + (1)($46,400) + (6)($33,800)]/15 = $32,233 closest to $32,000

12. 16½ - (4)(2'5³⁄₈") = 16'6" – 8'21½" = 16'6" – 9'9½" = 6'8½"

13. Annual savings = 12E – 52S

14. 7 ÷ ¾ = $9.\overline{3}$, which means each interviewer can interview a maximum of 9 applicants each day. Then, (5)(9)(15) = 675 applicants

15. 4800/(4800+6400) = 3/7 eligible. On that assumption, there would be (3/7)(14,000) = 6000 eligible applicants. Then, 1200/6000 = 20%

16. 266 – (3)(76) = 38 gallons of oil left. Then, 38/76 = ½ hour

17. (6)(7)(4) = 168 hours to check on 336 tenants. This means 2 tenants require 1 man-hour. Now, (6)(7)(x days) = man-hours would be needed to check the remaining 420 tenants. This requires 210 man-hours. So, (6)(7)(x) = 210. Solving, x = 5

18. $\frac{17.5}{25}$ = .7 hr. = 42 min. Total time = 42 + 15 = 57 minutes.

19. Number available = 320[1−.25(1/8)(.75) = 210

20. Total cost = (.70)[(24)($3.60)+(4)(27.50)] = $137.48

21. From January through April, amount = (8)($185+$53+$17.50+$22) + (4)($550) = $4420. From May through December, amount = (16)($185+$53+17.50+$22) + (8)($550)(1.12) = $9368. Total annual amount = $4420 + $9368 = $13,788

22. Meat allowance = ($400)(.30)(1.10) = $132; fruit and vegetable allowance = ($400)(.30)(.80) = $96; grocery allowance = ($400)(.25)(1.05) = $105; dairy allowance = ($400)(.15) = $60. New monthly allowance = $132 + $96 + $105 + $.60 = $393

23. From January through May, amount = (10)($195+$63+$27.50+$32) + (5)($510) = $5725. From June through December, amount = (14)($195+$63+$27.50+$32) + (7)($510)(1.12) = $8443.40. Total annual amount = $5725 + $8443.40 = $14,168.40

24. Monthly assistance should be reduced to $600 − [(40)(3)($4^{1}/_{3}$) − ($5)(3)($4^{1}/_{3}$)] = $145. So, the semi-monthly amount is now $145/2 = $72.50

25. ($75)($4^{1}/_{3}$)/2 = original semi-monthly rent.
New semi-monthly rent = (162.50)(1.12) = $182. Since this represents an increase of $19.50, the new semi-monthly grant will be increased to $375 + $19.50 = $394.50

HUMAN RELATIONS

TABLE OF CONTENTS

	Page
INTRODUCTION	1
FACTS ABOUT PEOPLE	1
FACTS ABOUT RACE	2
RESPONSIBILITY OF GOVERNMENT	2
HUMAN RELATIONS UNDER STRESS	3
BEHAVIOR IN DISASTER	4
EFFECTS OF DISRUPTION OF LIVING HABITS	4

HUMAN RELATIONS

INTRODUCTION

The success of any enterprise is largely determined by its people: Their individual competences, the values they hold, and the quality of their leadership. This generalization stresses attributes important in business, industry, government, or institutional operations, the lack of which produces, at the least, inefficiency and, at the worst, disruption or even destruction of enterprises.

Disaster and civil defense emergency conditions complicate the effective use of personnel, the attainment of objectives, and the control of the citizenry in the affected areas. Normal interpersonal and intergroup relations tend to deteriorate and individual, group, and community effectiveness is lost.

Most of us recognize that understanding and practicing good human relations is important under normal circumstances, but under ordinary conditions most interpersonal adjustments are made simply, easily, and often unconsciously. They are habituated responses learned, practiced, and found effective during countless repetitions of personal contacts. Effective human relations under emergency conditions, however, may be more difficult and their attainment becomes a serious matter for study and understanding.

The phrase "human relations" includes subject matter almost as broad as the study of mankind itself. Many books have been written on the subject. In this brief chapter we can deal only summarily with a few of the more important concepts involved in relations among human beings.

FACTS ABOUT PEOPLE

It is a truism that people are alike in some ways but different in other ways. Handling human relations situations wisely requires sensitivity to individual differences. Physically some people are short and some tall, some fat and some thin. Some adhere to one religion, some to another, and some to none. One person may never have gone to school while his neighbor may have had six years or more of college. Yet the former may be wealthy and the latter relatively poor. One may be an outcast in his neighborhood, one well liked, and still another socially prominent. The first may be a gentle recluse and the last aggressive and domineering. More than likely each of us in large measure reflects the attitudes of our parents or, if we have grown away from these, of a group of our peers. There can be no doubt that we are products of both our heredity and our environment. The interrelationship of various facets of both determine what we are physically, intellectually, and emotionally.

We must recognize that each of us is an individual. Each has his own physique, level of intelligence, special skills and problems, and his own set of beliefs, and prejudice. The latter may include either fear or contempt of the law. Knowing people and recognizing their differences, their strong points and weaknesses, will make us more effective as we attempt to handle emergency conditions and to achieve a measure of normalcy.

While no simple set of "how to" rules can be formulated which will fit all, or even most, human relations situations, a good general principle to keep in mind is the Golden Rule: "Do unto others as you would that they should do unto you"—to which we might add the corollary: *If you had their individual differences.* Therefore, to apply this principle, you will need to study people, and especially their *differences* to be able to "put yourself in the other person's place."

FACTS ABOUT RACE

The term race has many meanings to many people. To some it simply means a group of people descended from a common ancestry and consisting of persons who have similar *physical characteristics*. It is in this sense that many speak of whites, Indians, or black. Others tend to think of races in terms of *nationalities*, such as Italians, Greeks, or Norwegians, insofar as these names denote people coming from various countries or cultures. When majority and minority groups live side by side, a person who essentially is similar to those of the majority, but who has a trace of the minority group characteristics frequently is grouped with the latter. Even competent anthropologists are not in agreement about what constitutes a race and what distinguishes one race from another. Mingling of human stock has gone on throughout recorded history and relative distinctions based on so-called racial characteristics (such as color of skin, hair, etc.) continue to become more obscure.

It is significant that no basic psychological differences between so-called races have been scientifically established. Superficial differences do exist, tend to become exaggerated, and produce commonly accepted stereotypes. It can, in fact, be reasonably concluded that greater psychological differences exist among people of each race than exist among races.

Superiority of one race over another, long an emotional crutch for the personally inadequate and a rallying cry to international and economic conflict, simply cannot be demonstrated. Like it or not, depending on our personal convictions, it can honestly be said that we are "brothers under the skin."

To be very specific, the "knowledge" we commonly hold about race is really an expression of attitudes that we have come to accept and a product of what we have learned to believe.

Relearning some of one's early conditioning about race or learning to minimize it or compensate for it, is necessary for many people if they are to function effectively in situations involving relations with people of other "races."

RESPONSIBILITY OF GOVERNMENT

For government to serve its purpose fully, it must not only apply the law equally and without favoritism, but it must also provide equal protection and service to all. This position can be accepted as an essential principle of the American creed. Nonetheless, diligent effort must always be applied to make this principle a fact of life to all of our people. Therefore, the law itself must be the rule by which we live and work. There can be no fact of a citizen's makeup— color, religion, or economic or social status—that will change his relative position under the law. Poor man, beggar, merchant or thief, although they may conduct themselves differently and hold different beliefs, are each entitled to a common application of the law. It thus becomes imperative that while on duty the individual officer submerge any of his prejudices and beliefs which are contrary to the law and contrary to the above principle. The most critical factor in producing such professional, objective law enforcement action is that he not bend the law to enforce his own code of conduct or utilize his authority out of spite against those who have antagonized him personally.

The police agency's protection and service must be allocated equally and applied freely to all. The agency serves all of the people and neither the status of an individual citizen nor an officer's attitude toward him should influence the agency's kind or level of service.

This composite result of all our interpersonal and interagency contacts is essentially based on job performance and the competence of the agency and of each employee. This refers not only to specific goals which are attained but also to the method by which they are attained and the conduct of all participating employees. An image of an agency gained through a formal public relations program can at best be of only superficial value if it does not reflect the actual worth of the agency. This, in essence, is the distinction between reputations and character. Reputation based on sound characters has lasting value; reputation otherwise based in transient and of dubious value.

There must be a thorough knowledge of human relations by personnel of all ranks. The practice of sound and understanding human relations is bound to strengthen and deepen the department's public relations and to give it lasting character.

Subordination of the officer's personal biases, prejudices, and beliefs to the policy of the department is essential in the handling of incidents and people. If an officer believes his own position is right, but is contrary to that of the agency, he may properly attempt to persuade his superiors to his point of view. He must recognize, however that so long as the agency policy continues, he must conform to it meticulously.

It is simpler to prescribe and require conformity to regulations and procedures which influence public relations than it is to change a man's basic beliefs. If agency policy is based on human understanding, common sense requires that it not only be understood, but also accepted: hence the importance of personnel training in both human relations and public relations.

HUMAN RELATIONS UNDER STRESS

Although human relations to the stress of emergency conditions will vary, they will tend to follow the pattern which is normal to each individual. Individual adjustment to circumstances is usually rapid and effective. Within his own limitations and capabilities each individual will attempt to "carry on." Most will respond to effective leadership and under such leadership may be expected to perform reasonably well under whatever circumstances arise.

However, if one person "panics" or loses control of himself while in the company of others, there is a tendency for his behavior to communicate itself to those about him. There is, therefore, an immediate need to identify any one who shows signs of such behavior. Two courses are then open. First, the person may simply be isolated. This will avoid the contagious effect. Second, he may be given treatment that may involve the use of sedatives on a doctor's orders; other medical measures; use of a psychiatrist, if circumstances permit; supportive efforts of lay persons who can assist the disturbed person to reorient himself. For example, this may sometimes be accomplished by giving him work to do which occupies his mind and reduces his apprehensions. The person who emotionally seeks a scapegoat may also be a source of serious problems. If he is of a dominating nature, he may quickly rally to his "cause" many others who are seeking emotional release, a sense of self-importance, and group identification. Such measures as isolation and treatment may be necessary to minimize his harmful influence.

It is to be expected that there will be some unusual human reactions in time of civil defense emergency or other major disaster that can be considered quite normal. We may expect that these would be manifested in forms less serious than those which we have been discussing. For example, there may be increased muscular tension and bodily responses, and some accompanying psychological manifestations such as excitement and confusion. It is to be stressed, however, that such conditions as a certain stiffness of movement, heavy perspiration, rapid breathing, sudden talkativeness, or unusual quiet are all normal reactions to unusual conditions.

Disaster reactions become abnormal and can be classified as disaster fatigue only when the kinds of conditions indicated above do not pass away quickly and spontaneously without treatment. If a person does not lose or quickly regains his effectiveness, his reaction may be considered normal.

Mild disaster fatigue normally will soon pass without treatment and with no ill effects. It is not usually a concern to emergency personnel except as it somewhat reduces a person's effectiveness. However, if it does not disappear or becomes slightly more severe, we may classify it as moderate disaster fatigue. If the fatigue does not pass or if it tends to become progressively more severe, treatment is indicated and persons so affected should have medical attention. In the case of severe fatigue, medical attention is mandatory. Unless medical service is promptly available, the person may be past susceptibility to treatment and quick recovery. Immediate medical treatment may return persons to normal, prevent increased fatigue and loss of effectiveness, and avoid unusual problems of prolonged care and treatment.

BEHAVIOR IN DISASTER

Concern of civil authorities with people extends, in time, from the normal conditions before disaster to the relatively stable conditions finally achieved after the disaster, whether or not they, in fact, resemble the normal predisaster conditions. It is important to remember that it is during the predisaster normal conditions people must be prepared for disaster. This includes preparing individuals to anticipate disaster conditions, and to accept group organization and training to minimize its effects.

In adequate indoctrination and training have been provided, the warning phase should pose no special problems, but should be a period in which official disaster plans can be placed in effect with individuals taking predetermined precautions, or proceeding to designated posts. Emergency personnel should be on the alert for signs of panic or other disturbances, and be prepared to take appropriate actions.

The impact phase is a critical one because of its disruption of the community and its normal activities. Power may be lost, transportation may break down, and entire geographic areas may be physically isolated or destroyed. This period will be a serious test of plans, organization, uncertainty, and confusion. Persons will have disaster fatigue in all of its manifestations and degrees. Big problems will demand attention and action. As the postimpact phase is entered, recovering from the effects of the disaster will move toward the resumption of normalcy. At this point, special attention must be given to problems of disaster fatigue, prompt treatment provided for those in need, and accommodations provided for those who may require extended care. Many who survive the critical emergency period may now have delayed emotional reactions, and attention must be given to identifying these people and providing them with necessary care.

EFFECTS OF DISRUPTION OF LIVING HABITS

Living in a shelter or relocation area will be an experience with which the average person can draw no comparison from his experience. Unless he has been in military service, or in prison, it will probably be his first experience as an adult in living closely with others not of his own choice. Under these circumstances he cannot simply "be himself." There must be provided effective patterns of group living and he must learn to adjust to them. He will remain an individual, but he must accept a unique responsibility for self-subordination to group goals and conduct. It must be recognized that this, for many, will be difficult, and it must be given due weight by leaders and their staff to induce harmonious, cooperative, and productive patterns of group living.

A special problem will be the presence of many persons separated from members of their families. Sometimes this will be the heartbreaking and final separation of death, and at other times perhaps even more emotion-laden situation of uncertainty about loved ones. Every effort must be made to keep together, or to reunite, members of families.

Other problems will be created by the presence, in some cases, of criminals, drug addicts, and other deviates. The exigencies of group living may well result in magnification of problems of "normal people which are more manageable in normal living. For example, tobacco smokers will need to be controlled for the welfare of all of the inhabitant of a shelter. Habitual smokers deprived of their regular gratification, whether because of shelter rules or because their supply of tobacco is exhausted, will experience discomfort or hardship, and may be irritable. Sexual advances may take place which would not be likely in the same group of people if they were gathered together under more normal circumstances.

Most persons, in establishing their own patterns of living seek harmonious relationships. This often means that people group themselves in communities where there are common backgrounds of race, nationality, religion, education, and employment. Living under emergency conditions, will seldom allow this. People who do not know or "understand" each other will find themselves living closely together under conditions of privation and hardship. In such circumstances, adjustment may be difficult.

In an emergency, there is enforced restriction or mobility. People cannot get away from others whom they would not normally choose as companions. Again, for this reason, everyone must accept unusual responsibilities for harmonious and cooperative living, and leaders must make every effort to minimize frictions imposed by the lack of mobility.

For all practical purposes, normal pursuits will not be available to more than a few. Leaders must seek out opportunities to keep people productively occupied both as individuals and as groups.

The above considerations suggest that leaders and their staff, including law enforcement personnel, will need to be capable of diagnosing and managing human relations situations within the group. Fortunately, research in human behavior provides much in the way of guidelines for such an endeavor, and Federal DCPA courses afford opportunities for leaders and their staffs to increase their capabilities in such matters.

In spite of all of the problems, leaders must keep living conditions as bearable as possible. Since no single way of living will be normal for anyone, the problems of personal adjustment and group leadership will be difficult. Accordingly, leaders have to be on the alert constantly to anticipate difficulties of interpersonal and intergroup relations in time to take preventive action. Avoidance of group tensions and conflict is by far the better course of action than attempts to correct or overcome problem situations once they have developed.

It is a first responsibility of leadership to give confidence to those in the group. While this confidence may sometimes result from an outstanding "natural leader," it is more often the result of a studied effort to build it. The people must be kept as well informed as possible about what is going on in the disaster area.

Leaders must organize and direct activities which may be productive or divertive in nature, but must be meaningful to those who participate. Leaders must be honest about problems, positive in their actions, and impartial and humane in carrying out their decisions. The kind of leadership exerted will largely determine community morale and smoothness of the transition back to more nearly normal living.

6

www.ingramcontent.com/pod-product-compliance
Lightning Source LLC
Chambersburg PA
CBHW082211300426
44117CB00016B/2766